Pasta!

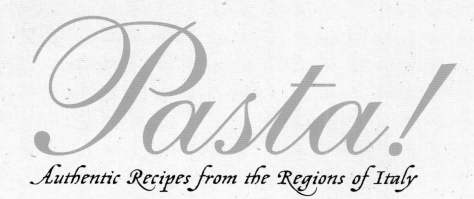

Pasta!

Authentic Recipes from the Regions of Italy

Text and Recipes by Pamela Sheldon Johns

Produced by Jennifer Barry Design

Photography by Joyce Oudkerk-Pool

Ten Speed Press
Berkeley • Toronto

A Kirsty Melville Book

Ten Speed Press
Box 7123, Berkeley, California 94707
www.tenspeed.com

Distributed in Australia by Simon & Schuster Australia, in Canada by Ten Speed Press Canada,
in New Zealand by Southern Publishing Group, in South Africa by Real Books, in Southeast Asia
by Berkeley Books, and in the United Kingdom and Europe by Airlift Books.

Concept and Design: Jennifer Barry Design, Sausalito, California
Production Assistant: Kristen Wurz
Copy Editor: Barbara King
Food Stylist: Pouké
Prop Stylist: Carol Hacker/Tableprop

Library of Congress Cataloging-in-Publication Data
Johns, Pamela Sheldon, 1953–
Pasta! : authentic recipes from the regions of Italy / text and recipes by Pamela Sheldon Johns ;
produced by Jennifer Barry Design ; photography by Joyce Oudkerk-Pool.
p.   cm.
Includes index.
ISBN 1-58008-264-5
1. Cookery (Pasta) 2. Cookery, Italian. I. Title.
TX809.M17 J65   2001
641.8'22--dc21   00-048918

Printed in Hong Kong
First printing, 2001
1 2 3 4 5 6 7 8 9 10 — 04 03 02 01

Contents

Introduction

"She must be Neapolitan!" laughs our waiter in a cozy Naples restaurant. I look over at my toddler, who is lifting handfuls of spaghetti to her mouth with her fingers. The waiter then points to a classic painting on the wall, a street scene from early Naples when vendors sold pasta on the streets, and consumers lifted the steaming noodles to their mouths with two fingers. Pasta has come a long way from this provincial slice of history. And yet, much remains the same.

Basic dried pasta is, after all, only flour and water. The way those two ingredients are handled can make all the difference in the taste and nutrition of this humble food. Industry has turned it into a product that can be found in much of the world, but a few artisanal producers still make it the way it was made in early Naples. The secret is in the use of quality durum (hard) wheat, good water, extrusion with bronze dies, and a long drying process. The result is a noodle that needs very little dressing to make it taste wonderful. A straightforward garnish of a good extra-virgin olive oil and a sprinkling of Parmigiano-Reggiano is simply divine.

From its roots in history, the culture of pasta spread over Italy like wildfire. In most regions today it is a staple. From its origins as a simple, inexpensive food that could nourish peasant workers, pasta has evolved to a high art. In most restaurants, the first course, or primo, is an indication of the quality of the rest of the meal. It's not just pasta . . . it's Italy's national dish.

History

Let's settle this right up front: While it is true that the Chinese history of pasta making dates back to 3000 B.C.E., historians do not credit the Venetian explorer Marco Polo for bringing pasta to Italy. As far back as the fourth century B.C.E., Etruscans carved reliefs depicting the culture and technique of pasta making in the vicinity of Rome. Some historians believe that pasta originated in the Arabic countries, a feasible hypothesis, because Mesopotamia is the birthplace of cultivated grain. In the first century C.E., in his book *De Re Coquinaria,* Roman historian Apicius describes an ancient Roman dish made of wide strips of fresh pasta layered with meat, fish, and eggs. The dish was called *lagano* or *laganella,* words that described wide strips of pasta, which may have evolved to the modern name, *lasagna.* It is not certain if this dough was baked, breadlike, in an oven or cooked in liquid, a distinguishing attribute of pasta. However, Apicius also discusses using broken pieces of fresh pasta to thicken soups.

According to historical documents from before the eleventh century (during Arabic migration), ships' logs reveal that pasta was dried to preserve it for travel. The pasta strips, called *tria,* or *itryia* (an Arabic word that originally defined strips of bread), were primarily from Palermo. Most likely this was made with hard wheat semolina, because common wheat could not have withstood the drying and transportation processes. The drying was carried out in the hot Sicilian sun and tempered in humid rooms (explained more fully on page 27). This method of preservation allowed traveling ships to spread pasta from port to port, and soon the innovation reached harbors in Genoa, Pisa, Amalfi, and Venice. Also, sailors took the Sicilian art of drying pasta from their voyages back home with them. Nancy Harmon Jenkins, author of *Flavors of Puglia,* describes a modern version of *itryia* in Puglia, "a wonderful dish called *'ciceri e tria.'* The fresh pasta noodles are made from semolina and water, with no egg. Two-thirds of the pasta is boiled as usual, then tossed with chickpeas. The rest of the pasta is deep-fried until crisp, then used as a garnish."

In the twelfth century, in a book by Arab geographer Idrìsi (1154), there is a description of mills in the settlement of Trabìa, Sicily, making pasta in such quantities that it was transported by ship to "Muslim and Christian" countries.

A document from 1279, an inventory of an inheritance that mentions a *bariscella piena de maccherone* (a basket full of macaroni), further supports the existence of pasta in Italy before Marco Polo. This was thirteen years before the explorer returned from China.

In these early times as the craft was developed, guilds formed to establish rules and regulations for the trade. The first guild was an association of bakers and pasta makers in Florence in 1337. Later, the groups formed according to the shapes and types of pasta: *fidelari* in Genoa and Savona; *vermicelli* in Naples, Palermo, and Rome; in Sicily, *maccaruni* (generic for long cylindrical pasta) and *trii* (the Sicilian word for spaghetti, and probably a descendant of *itryia*); and *lasagna* in Venice.

Now that the issue of Marco Polo is out of the way, we can discuss how pasta became Italy's national dish and, in four hundred years, evolved into more than three hundred shapes. It was a staple in Naples by the sixteenth century, but it wasn't until the eighteenth century that pasta became a commercial success. Before that, the hard wheat needed for pasta was grown only in Sicily and Puglia, making it an expensive commodity outside of those areas. Pasta was a dish for the wealthy, served as a treat or even for dessert. Throughout the seventeenth century, as the farmers near Naples began growing their own wheat, and as the screw-press pasta maker and kneading machines grew to be more practical, pasta from Campania became more economical and widely distributed, and went from being a food for the elite to one that could sustain the hardworking peasant.

The introduction of tomatoes from the Americas in the late 1700s was an important contribution to the success of pasta. The first mention of this delectable combination was in 1839 in Naples, in a recipe published in *Cucina Teorico Practica,* a cookbook by Ippolito Cavalcanti, Duke of Buonvicino.

In the early 1800s, three major ports shipped commercial dried pasta: Palermo (Sicily), Naples (Campania), and Genoa (Liguria). The durum wheat came primarily from Puglia, Sicily, and northern Africa, and the demand for such wheat was great enough to import some from Russia (near the Sea of Azov). Up until now the kneading, cutting of the dough, and extrusion were all done by hand. The pasta was left to dry in the sun and was subject to the ambient humidity.

Pasta workshops proliferated, and by 1890 there were more than two hundred factories in the vicinity of Genoa. Fresh pasta

was also very popular in the north and spread rapidly along the Po River and over the Padano plain. In the south, with the proximity of a grain-growing area and an excellent source of water, the towns of Gragnano and Torre Annunziata, near Naples, became the center of a major pasta industry. At the turn of the century, with the advent of electricity, industrial progress grew rapidly. Machinery that had been driven by hand or horse was replaced. Mechanical drying rooms allowed areas with less than favorable climate conditions to make pasta. Over the next twenty years the invention of labor- and time-saving equipment, such as semolina processors, kneaders, and hydraulic presses for extrusion, increased the volume and accessibility of the pasta to the lower classes. In the 1930s, a new system of production incorporated the mixing of the dough, kneading, and extrusion into one continuous process.

Today, the making of pasta can all be done with computers, yet some producers maintain the traditional elements that set an artisan pasta apart from an industrial one. The key fundamentals, notwithstanding selection of quality ingredients, are the use of bronze extrusion dies (perforated plates for shaping) and slow air drying.

Bronze dies give the extruded pasta a rough, porous external surface that helps sauce cling to it. Industrial producers, on the other hand, often use Teflon dies. Teflon is easier to clean and squirts out the pasta at a high speed, resulting in a pasta with a hard, slick finish that doesn't interact with sauces.

The second important issue, air drying, is important to the flavor of the pasta. Industrial producers flash-dry the pasta in high heat over a short time, two to four hours, a process that kills flavor. Artisanal air drying is done in warm rooms with constant air circulation, simulating the historic process of sun drying over a period of days.

There are important regional differences in pasta, related to local products and traditions. Northern regions predominated in fresh pasta because soft wheat flour was more available there. The rich agricultural areas of the north are inclined to make an egg-rich fresh pasta served with preparations that use their abundance of dairy products, such as cheese, butter, and cream. In the south, in the more historically impoverished areas, the tendency has been toward leaner dishes, such as eggless dried semolina pasta garnished with simple local ingredients, of olive oil, tomato, sheep's milk cheese, etc. Central Italy blends the northern and southern traditions, but actually has fewer original pasta shapes. (Bread plays a bigger role in the first courses of inland Tuscany and Umbria.) The coastal areas, however, have developed short, strong shapes that hold up well to seafood and vegetable sauces.

Still, although they have these differences, most regions make fresh egg pasta and most make dried semolina pasta. The fresh pasta is usually made with a soft wheat flour, sometimes with eggs and sometimes without. Dried pasta is made with a durum wheat flour, usually without eggs.

Spaghetti is probably the most popular cross-regional shape. Pasta shape names change from region to region. What Genova calls *farfalle* (butterfly or bowtie) in Bologna is also called *gasse*. Sometimes the name stays the same, but the recipe changes, such as *gnocchi*. In some regions it is made with potato, and in some it is not.

Generically, the term *macaroni* describes any number of long cylindrical shapes, whether solid or hollow, and *lasagna* refers to flat pasta of any width, but *macaroni* sometimes refers to all dry pasta. Some pasta shapes are found only in one area, such as *chiancarelle,* a small *orecchiette* named after the roofs of the *trulli* (ancient stone buildings) in Puglia.

Seasonal influences are reflected in pasta dishes. Pasta will provide the proper canvas when, for example, artichokes are in season in the spring, or porcini mushrooms spring up in the fall.

As in all good cooking, the quality of the ingredients reflects the outcome of the finished dish. The primary ingredient in pasta is ground wheat. The motto of the National Museum of Pasta in Rome says it very well: *Se la farina è argento, la semola è oro*—if flour is silver, semolina is gold.

Pasta by Shape

Pasta shapes can be categorized into five basic families:

LONG: with round compact cross section (for example, *spaghetti* or *spaghettini*); with a hollow central cross section (for example, *bucatini* or *fusilli*); with a flattened cross section (for example, *linguine* or *fettucine*)

SHORT: cut into short lengths (for example, *maccheroni* or *penne*)

SMALL: tiny shapes used in broths, such as *stelline* or *annelini*

STAMPED: cut from sheets of pasta, such as *farfalle* or *cravattine*

FOLDED: sheets that are folded and cut, such as *capelli d'angelo* or *tagliolini*

Pasta by the Regions of Italy

With more than three hundred identified shapes, it would be impossible to list everything. Here are a few of the more popular shapes.

NORTHERN ITALY

Bigoli *(Veneto/Friuli)*

Garganelli *(Emilia-Romagna)*

Gramigna *(Emilia-Romagna)*

Pizzoccheri *(Lombardia)*

Spaghetti lunghi
  (Veneto/Friuli)

Tagliatelle *(Emilia-Romagna)*

Tajarin al tartufo *(Piemonte)*

Tubettini rigati *(Lombardia)*

CENTRAL ITALY

Pappardelle *(Toscana)*

Pici *(Toscana)*

Spaghettone *(Toscana)*

Strangozzi *(Umbria)*

Trenette *(Liguria)*

Trofie *(Liguria)*

SOUTHERN ITALY

Bucatini *(Lazio)*

Candele *(Campania)*

Casareccia *(Campania)*

Cavatelli *(Basilicata)*

Cavatappi *(Abruzzo)*

Cencioni *(Basilicata)*

Chitarra *(Abruzzo)*

Cicatelli *(Puglia)*

Conchiglie *(Abruzzo)*

Farfalle *(Campania)*

Fettuccine *(Lazio)*

Fregula *(Sardegna)*

Fusilli lunghi *(Campania)*

Malloreddus/gnocchetti sardi
  (Sardegna)

Orecchiette *(Puglia)*

Pasta al ceppo *(Abruzzo)*

Penne *(Campania)*

Penne rigate *(Campania)*

Riccia *(Abruzzo)*

Rigatoni *(Lazio)*

Saittini/spaghetti al
  peperoncino *(Calabria)*

Spaghettini *(Campania)*

Strozzapreti *(Calabria)*

Taccozzette *(Abruzzo)*

Ziti *(Campania)*

Grains

In southern Italy, wheat has been cultivated since the fifth century B.C.E. One of the most ancient grains is *farro comune* (*Triticum dicoccum*), also called emmer. This grain dates back to Etruscan times in Italy, hundreds of years before the birth of Christ, but probably has its origins in Palestine. It is a hard wheat that works well in pasta. *Farro grande* (*triticum spelta*), the version of spelt that we see also in the United States, is a soft wheat variety and doesn't work well for pasta.

Farro was phased out during the Middle Ages when new varieties of wheat grain were cultivated. The new varieties had higher yields and were easier to harvest. Farro nearly became extinct until it gained a new popularity in recent years. Now, in the Tuscan area called Garfagnana, near Lucca, the hard variety is again a staple, found as a whole or cracked grain in soups, salads, or ground into flour. The berry is nutty in flavor and high in protein (up to 20 percent).

In the north, high-yield soft wheat flourished, used for breads and fresh pasta. The "new" wheat variety that squeezed out farro in the south was durum (hard) wheat, a grain suitable for preparing dried pasta. The major agricultural center of durum wheat was, and is, in Puglia at the edge of Abruzzo, on the plains around Foggia. With today's worldwide popularity of pasta, the farms are unable to produce enough. The grain is now supplemented with imports from Canada, Argentina, and the United States.

One family in the Marche region has been working to improve the durum wheat for pasta. Since 1888 the Latinis have farmed in Osimo, near Ancona. Not satisfied with local durum wheat, Carlo Latini and wife, Carla, have cultivated various hard-grain wheats since 1984 in search of the perfect pasta grain with a high protein content and a lot of flavor. Drawing from the work of agronomist Nazareno Strampelli, Latini has developed a strain he calls Senatore Cappelli. Even though this strain has a low production yield, the grain has up to 17 percent protein. From this small crop Latini produces only four shapes—*spaghetti, spaghettini, pennette,* and *spaghetti alla chitarra*—carrying the name Selezione Senatore Cappelli, one of my favorite dried *paste* (plural of Italian *pasta*).

Flour made from durum wheat is preferred for dried pasta because of its high protein, a quality that allows the gluten to develop. Gluten is created when liquid is added to the flour and agitation (kneading, mixing, stirring) occurs. The liquid activates the gliadin and glutenin, two elements found in the protein, and forms a structure containing starch granules. This structure gives strength and elasticity to the dough. In semola the gluten that is developed is stronger and shorter than common wheat, which enables it to tolerate stretching.

This is an important thing to know when you use flour in recipes. Even all-purpose flour is high enough in protein to develop gluten. If you are making bread or pasta, you want that gluten to develop so you knead and knead to get it very elastic. (In muffins and cakes, if you over mix the batter and the gluten develops, the result will be spongy. That is why their recipes will call for a softer flour, such as cake or pastry flour, or instruct you not to overmix the batter.)

Tipo oo is the silky white flour
used to make fresh pasta. It is lower
in protein than American all-purpose
flour, which is why I suggest
adding a little cake or pastry flour to
all-purpose flour when making
fresh pasta. In "The Italian Baker,"
Carol Field recommends using
one part pastry flour to three parts
all-purpose flour to approximate
Tipo oo flour, but you might want to
experiment to achieve the pasta
that suits your taste. See Resources,
page 108, for mail-order sources
of Tipo oo flour.

Milling

The milling of grains has a long history. In ancient times milling was done by hand with a mortar and pestle. By 25 B.C.E., a horse-powered mill had come into use in Rome. By the first century C.E., Roman architect Vitruvius had designed and built a water-powered mill that could adjust coarseness or fineness of the flour.

A few years ago I met Beppe Parigi, a miller in Loro Ciuffenna, Tuscany, who grinds tender grains in a mill that dates back to the 1100s. The mill is run by the force of the river running under it. Recently, I was pleased to find another water-powered mill in northern Tuscany at the edge of Emilia-Romagna. This mill, the Molino Ronci, is in Pontè Messa, at Pennabilli near San Marino. Since the 1500s, this has been the site of a water-powered mill. The Ronci

family has a small operation, milling local and imported grains for local families and restaurants. The water from the river enters the space two floors beneath the mill's working area where paddled waterwheels, *ritrecene,* drive the millstones. Molino Ronci only mills "tender" grains, such as corn for polenta or the soft local wheat for baking and pasta. Once milled, the flour is filtered through a screen to separate the bran and chaff, then weighed and bagged to sell.

In the small town of Moscufo, near Pescara in Abruzzo, the mill Molino Cappelli grinds, with more modern processes, organic farro. Cesare and Vincenzo Cappelli use a stone for grinding that is hard, yet porous, with grooves along the surface. The speed that the wheel turns is crucial to the outcome of the flour. At about 100 rpm (revolutions per minute), they run at one-third the rate of industrial mills. The slower speed keeps the grain from overheating, a process that preserves flavor, smell, and nutrients.

In Italy, ground soft wheat is called *farina,* or flour; ground durum wheat is called *semola;* the finely ground version is *semolina.* What we buy in the United States is called *semolina,* but is actually closer to *semola,* the coarsely ground type used in Italy for pasta. The semolina we see for sale in the United States is sometimes labeled "pasta flour." It is true; by law this is the flour used in commercial dried pasta in Italy. But it is almost never used in fresh pasta—the result would be a very tough noodle. Rather, soft wheat flour, such as our all-purpose flour, creates a tender, but toothsome pasta. In Italy, fresh pasta is made with soft wheat flour, with the possible exception of some homemade pasta, such as *orecchiette,* in the south where the local wheat is durum.

Italians grade flour according to the refining process, rather than the American system of rating by protein content. Tipo 00 is the most refined and contains the least fiber. Tipo 0 has had 70 percent of the fiber removed; Tipo 1 and Tipo 2 have increasing amounts of husk and germ; and *integrale* uses the whole wheat berry and varies only in the consistency of the coarseness of milling.

Fresh Pasta: Ravioli and Fusilli

I don't go south of Naples without going to see my friend Cecilia Baratta Bellelli. We stay on her *agriturismo,* a working farm that allows guests, near Paestum, the Magna Grecian ruins south of Salerno. She raises water buffalo in the wet lowlands of the Sele River, and on her table appear wonders made from their milk. Cecilia has introduced me to some of my most memorable food moments—not only at the table, but also in the mountains and on the plains of her homeland. On a recent visit she took me to see Giuseppina Maffia at her shop in Capaccio Scalo.

Inspired by the buffalo mozzarella that is prepared at her back door, Signora Maffia has sold pasta from her shop for six years. She has been making pasta for as long as she can remember, learning her art from her grandmother, a skill that is evident in her comfort in handling the dough. The shop is called La Casereccia, which means "home-style." She sells fewer than twenty different shapes in total, but each day she offers only two or three freshly made shapes with the help of her sister-in-law, Francesca Sabia. The shapes are labor-intensive ones that must be done by hand, such as the local *orecchiette,* called *strascinati,* curly *fusilli,* or the fresh *gnocchi.* The only colored pasta is an elongated oval, colored green with spinach, named *foglie di ulivo,* "olive leaves."

Signora Maffia's specialty is her luscious ravioli filled with the local buffalo milk ricotta cheese. The six styles she artfully makes are a generous 3-inch round *cappellaccio,* a pyramid-like *cestello,* a small square *agnolotto,* a triangular *triangolo,* a small round *raviolo,* and her signature raviolo, the *casereccio,* a one-half- by three-inch rectangle. All of the *ravioli* have fluted edges.

Signora Maffia's basic recipe for fresh pasta dough is three and a half ounces (one hundred grams) of Tipo 00 (soft wheat) flour and one whole egg for each serving. The buttery yellow color of her pasta dough reflects the brilliant yolk of her fresh, local eggs. At home and for small special orders, she mixes and rolls the dough out by hand. She cracks the eggs into a well in the center of the mound of flour and gradually works the eggs into the dough with her fingertips, incorporating the flour a little at a time. In the shop, to keep up with her business, she uses a mixer and rolls the sheets of pasta out by machine.

I can see that much of the work is still done by hand as she demonstrates making the *ravioli.* The long sheets are stretched out on the wooden table and dotted at regular intervals with the filling mixture of ricotta, Parmigiano-Reggiano, sometimes cooked and chopped spinach, and a little salt. A second sheet of pasta dough is placed on top, and with her fingers, Signora Maffia presses out the air and creates a seal in between each of the mounds of filling. She is then ready to cut the shapes. For the straight-sided shapes (square, rectangle, or triangle), she uses a fluted pastry wheel, and with practiced precision, quickly cuts the shape with the plump mound in the center and a quarter-inch edge around it. She stamps the round shapes out by hand. She slides the finished *ravioli* onto flour-dusted trays and places them in her display case for sale. In no time at all the locals have emptied the case.

I asked her to show me how the curly *fusilli* is made, with the center hollow like a straw. She starts with a one- by four-inch strip of pasta that she rolls with the palm of her hand around a fine stick. In Signora Maffia's case, a rib from a former umbrella is a durable and appropriately sized tool. It looked easy until I tried my hand at it. By the time I had made five pieces, she had finished a trayful!

Orecchiette

Last summer in Puglia, early in the morning, as I walked around the *agriturismo* Masseria Salamina (see Resources, page 108), I saw Natalizia Rosato tending the goats and sheep. As she gently herded them into their pen to milk them, some of them, in their hurry to get in, jumped over the small fence like sheep in a dream. That night I would enjoy a dinner that included cheese made from their rich milk.

Masseria Salamina is in the heart of the dreamlike land of the *trulli,* surreal stone buildings that date back to the tenth century. It is in the countryside near a small town called Pezze di Greco, which literally means "pieces of the Greek," hinting at the ancient roots of the area. *Masseria* means farm, and while the residence looks like a castle to me, the owners call it a "seventeenth-century fortified farmhouse," built like a castle to defend against the Saracens. The 70 hectares (about 173 acres) are home to goats, sheep, hens, and rabbits against a backdrop of abundant olives, almonds, and citrus. This rocky land of Puglia has an austere beauty, quaint and untouched in many ways.

For the last fifteen years the *masseria* has been an *agriturismo.* Owner Anna Luigia Leone offers rooms that are spacious, the welcome is sweet, and the food is homemade and wonderful. Signora Leone invited me into the kitchen to watch Natalizia Rosato make the local pasta, *orecchiette,* for our lunch.

Here in Puglia, the home of hard wheat, the *orecchiette* and *cavatelli* are made with 100 percent hard wheat. Overall, the use of hard wheat flour in fresh pasta is the exception. The dough is hard to work by hand, and the pasta has a different consistency. The taste is satisfying and substantial, especially when cooked properly. The *orecchiette* are chewy and almost nutty, heavenly when combined in the classic dish Orecchiette con Cime di Rape (page 103), using fresh local greens.

With few words Natalizia put a mound of yellow *grano duro* (semolina) on the wooden board. She made a well in the center, poured in cold water, and began working the water into the semolina with her fingers. Then she began the hard work of kneading. After seeing her working with the sheep in the morning, she seems out of place to me in this stainless steel kitchen, but when she starts to knead, the surroundings disappear. The butter-yellow dough is strong and resistant, and Natalizia's strong hands push and pull it until it is smooth. She sets the dough aside to rest while she puts a large pot of water to boil.

To shape the *orecchiette*, which means "little ears," Natalizia cuts off a piece of dough and rolls it into a rope one-half inch thick. With a knife she cuts coin-sized slices that she smears across a rough wooden board with a flat-bladed table knife.

Then she turns it over her thumb to make a bulge that will serve to hold sauce. The rough board that she works on gives the *orecchiette* a coarse surface that helps hold sauce, too.

I had to try my hand at it. The first disk that I smeared curled up like a little taco. "No," Natalizia smiled. "If you press too hard, they become *cavatelli*."

In the same lesson I also learned that if they are too flat they become *stacchjoddi*. So all is not lost after all—I can make three shapes at once!

Maccheroni alla Chitarra

Between the mountains and the sea in Pianella, not far from a town auspiciously named Penne, my friend Gianluigi Peduzzi introduced me to Luciana di Giandomenico, an expert at making *maccheroni alla chitarra*. Three years ago, I received my best party tool from Gianluigi. It was a beautiful *chitarra*. *Chitarra* means "guitar," and this pasta-making instrument looks like a guitar, with a rectangular wooden frame strung with wires. I call it a party tool because I often have friends over for pasta parties. I make the dough ahead of time and they make the shapes they want to eat. Some make *ravioli*, some make *tortellini*, and some use the *chitarra* to make the classic Abruzzese pasta.

In Abruzzo, I learned that when Luciana makes her pasta with the *chitarra* she uses a lot of flour to keep it from sticking. The dough is made with a mixture of hard durum and soft wheat flour. She rolls out pieces to about a quarter inch thick, places a sheet on top of the *chitarra*, then rolls it with a rolling pin to press the dough through the wires, creating long noodles. Her *chitarra* is like mine, with the wires about a quarter inch apart. Sometimes Luciana makes a larger version called *rintrocili* by simply using a thicker sheet of dough. Some *chitarre* have the strings very close together to make *spaghetti alla chitarra* or wider to make ribbons.

Luciana was still making pasta when Giuseppina d'Annibale stepped in to show us how to make *frascarelli*. "This is the dish that mothers eat when nursing a baby," she explained. "It helps them have plenty of milk." I am certain that she was inspired to share this recipe because her son Giancarlo and his wife, Stefania, have a new baby girl, Judizia. I had been watching all of the women passing the little angel from arm to arm, and I could see that she didn't want for attention.

Signora d'Annibale puts a mound of flour on the worktable and sprinkles water over the flour with a little broom (photo page 21). The broom allows droplets of water to be dispensed over the flour without saturating it excessively. Working with her fingers, she rubs the dough over her palms and between her fingers to make little balls. These are then passed through a wide-mesh sieve to remove the loose flour.

I had to admit to her that I was a little skeptical about how this flour and water mixture could help a mother with lactation. "Believe me, it works," she answered. "You sauté tomato, garlic, and peperoncino in olive oil to put on top of the pasta, which has been cooked in boiling salted water for three to four minutes, until it is the consistency of polenta. Don't ask me why. It works."

Signora d'Annibale's son Giancarlo and his brother-in-law Gianluigi Peduzzi eat pasta every day. And why shouldn't they? They produce one of my favorite dried *paste,* Rustichella d'Abruzzo.

Dried Pasta

After watching the women work their magic with the fresh pasta, Gianluigi took me to his "new factory with the old equipment," to see the beginning of the dried pasta process. Gianluigi Peduzzi oversees the business started by his great-grandfather, Rafaele Sergiacomo, in nearby Penne. Sergiacomo was a miller who used a water-powered mill and was the first to have an electric mill. The pasta making business began with Gianluigi's grandfather, Gaetano Peduzzi, in the 1930s. Since 1981, when he began working with his father Piero, Gianluigi has carried on his family's tradition. Now, with his brother-in-law Giancarlo d'Annibale, they have created a thriving business in artisan pasta.

Making the Dough

The selection of the grain for dried pasta is of utmost importance. Also, at Rustichella, the flour is always milled no more than twenty-four hours before using it to make dough. In the late 1700s and early 1800s, the *gramolatura,* or kneading, of the semolina with boiling water was done by foot in a *madia,* a long wooden trough. Eventually a kneading machine, called a *gramola,* was introduced.

The amount of water needed depends upon the inherent moistness of the grain, which results from the humidity in the air when it was harvested, the method of storage, and the current day's humidity. It takes the experience of a traditional producer to determine these factors.

Nothing else is added, not even salt. Italian law forbids the addition of any preservatives or artificial coloring. When the dough is thoroughly mixed and kneaded, it is passed under pressure to remove any air bubbles that would cause inconsistency in the finished product.

Extruding and Shaping

The dough moves at once to the *trafilatura,* or extrusion. Historically, the *torchio* was the press used to push the dough through the die, powered by a screw or lever mechanism. Now the whole process (except the drying) is done completely in one machine. The only thing that changes is the bronze die that shapes the dough. The dough continues to move through the machine under pressure, to keep air bubbles from forming. Industrial producers use such high pressure that it can cause the dough to heat up, so they cool the die with water.

Gianluigi's grandfather created his bronze dies. There are hundreds of them, each designed to make a unique shape. *Conchiglie,* or shells, for example, are forced through an arc that causes the shape to curl as it drops out. Tube shapes have a round hole with a pin in the center. As the dough exits the die in its designated shape, it is cut with a knife. Bolognese pasta, such as *farfalle,* is stamped from extruded sheets.

In another part of Italy, according to Mario and Dino Martelli, if it's Friday, it must be spaghetti. It has been that way in the charming medieval Tuscan village of Lari (near Pisa) since

1926 when their grandfather, Guido Martelli, and his brother Gastone bought this *pastificio* (pasta factory) from Catellani, a producer that had been in that location since the end of the 1800s. The closeknit Martelli family carefully controls the consistently high quality of their pasta by keeping the business small. And it is a very small production, making approximately 10 quintals (about 2,200 pounds) per day using the manual methods that date back to the beginning of the Martelli business. The whole family participates in all aspects of the production, including Mario's twenty-one-year-old son, Lorenzo, and his two sisters, Valentina and Chiara. The chores are divided and shared: One oversees the making of the dough, the extrusion, and the drying; another manages the packaging; and another handles sales and marketing. Their pasta has all of the earmarks of an artisan product: high-quality Canadian durum that is milled nearby, the use of bronze dies, and slow, natural drying. They only make four classic shapes, inspired from an ancient Neapolitan catalog: Monday, Thursday, and Saturday are the days for *spaghettini* and *pasta corta* (*penne* and *maccherone*); Tuesday and Friday is *spaghetti;* and Wednesday is packaging day.

I arrived on Friday to see the spaghetti production. Their bronze dies have round holes from which the dough is forced under pressure. As the pasta emerges through the holes, it forms long strands and hangs down to form a curtain. A rod moves behind the strands. At the die plate the spaghetti is cut with a

sharp blade. The spaghetti is draped over canes and sent to dry for forty-eight to fifty hours, depending on the external conditions. Once finished, it rests in wooden containers until it is finally packaged by hand (on Wednesday) in their cheery yellow paper bags.

Their mix is 70 percent semolina, 30 percent water. They use less water because the climate is less dry here. They mix the dough more slowly and extrude it with less compression than some producers, giving a more porous dough that holds the sauce better. The porosity also helps the pasta to absorb more water when it cooks, giving an excellent yield.

Drying

As it is extruded, the Martelli pasta is automatically dropped onto drying trays that move to racks, ready for the next phase, drying.

Air drying is essential to the flavor of the pasta. A study done in 1987 found that higher temperatures in the drying process will destroy not only the flavor, but the nutritional values as well. The study pointed out that using high temperatures will allow the industrial pasta manufacturer to use poor-quality grains and flour. Artisanal producers use rooms heated to 40° to 45°C (77° to 86°F) with constant air circulation, simulating the historic process of sun drying. This lengthy drying, up to sixty hours long depending on the pasta's size and shape, helps to maintain the flavor, while removing the water that could cause it to spoil. The finished pasta, by law, must have 12.5 percent or lower moisture content.

The humidity of the air changes at different stages of the process. In the first phase, the air is drier and forms a hardened surface layer on the pasta that maintains the shape. After that the atmosphere becomes humid for a slower dehydration. The humidity helps prevent cracking. In historic times, the heat of the sun performed *incartamento,* the first intense drying. The pasta was then moved to a damp cool cellar for *rinvenimento,* or tempering, to allow the humidity to redistribute throughout the pasta. The final drying was in well-ventilated drying attics or sheltered courtyards. In those days, it took from eight to thirty days to complete the drying process. Naples had the perfect weather conditions for this process.

In the village of Castel San Giorgio, near Naples, Mario and Luigi Vicidomini carry on the work of their father, Raimondo, in a pasta-making business that began in 1812. Along with their brother-in-law, Aniello Rainone, the three men work over twelve hours a day in what is surely one of the oldest pasta workshops in Italy. Amazingly, they produce 150 varieties of pasta.

In the *cella cirillo,* a drying room from the 1940s, the pasta hangs from wooden dowels to dry. It is an understatement to say that it is hot in the room, which is not made any cooler by the gentle breeze of the wooden airplane propeller that moves the sultry air around. The time the pasta spends in this inferno depends on its shape and size. "It is important to dry it slowly," explains Mario Vicidomini. "The intense heat used in industrial pasta kills the gluten and the flavor. Our *tagliatelle* will stay in this room for three days; the larger *candele* takes five." The slow dehydrating process simulates the ambience of Castel San Giorgio's unrelenting sun, reminiscent of the days when the pasta was laid outside in this sunny province of Campania.

Gerardo Liguori, a family friend who sells the Vicidomini pasta to small local businesses, comes from a family who also had a very old *pastificio.* He reminisces, "When we were boys, our job was to watch the pasta drying in the streets. We had to chase the goats away! Vicidomini still makes pasta the way we did then, using the best semola from Altamura and our good mountain water. You can't compare it to what the modern factories are making—that stuff tastes like lupini." (It's an obscure analogy, but poignant. Lupini were beans that were dried and ground during the war when there was no flour; it was a preparation that sustained life, but had very little flavor.)

The Vicidomini machines are now sixty to sixty-five years old, presumably new in Raimondo's era. This is a very hands-on operation; the *linguini* is cut with scissors as it is extruded. One of my favorite shapes is the *calamari,* rings that look just like slices of the small squid. The Vicidominis make the classics including *candele,* a very long tube that looks like a candle. Using the semola of local durum wheat, they can produce 20 quintals (about 4,400 pounds) a day.

Luckily, we can now get several artisanal dried *paste* imported from Italy. Martelli, Latini, and Rustichella d'Abruzzo products are imported to most parts of the United States, or are available by mail order (see Resources, page 108). Other producers worth mentioning are Benedetto Cavalieri, Il Trullo: Sapori di Puglia, Gianfranco Zaccagni, Mamma Angelica, Cav. Giuseppe Cocco, Dallari, Michele Portoghese, and Settaro.

Some industrial dried pasta producers still tip their hat to traditional methods. Some have become multinational corporations, and some are no longer Italian-owned. The big names include Agnesi, Buitoni, Barilla, De Cecco, and Delverde.

Since 1824, Agnesi has been based in Imperia, in the very northern reaches of Liguria, near France. They were taken over by a French majority in 1990. Since that time, the family has set up a foundation and created the National Museum of Pasta in Rome (in 1993) to promote knowledge about Italian pasta, encourage research, and promote the use of pasta to reduce world hunger.

In 1827 Il Pastificio Buitoni opened the first major pasta manufacturing company. Barilla and Buitoni, the two largest Italian pasta companies, are vying for market dominance in the world's imported pasta.

De Cecco has produced pasta since 1887. They are one of the large producers that still use bronze dies, and their drying process is slower than most industrial manufacturers.

Making Pasta at Home

I have made so much fresh pasta that it is like second nature to me. Within thirty minutes, from flour to linguine, I can have a simple pasta on the table—less if I use a food processor to mix the dough. It seems so easy, and I can make it from ingredients that I always have on hand, that I never buy fresh pasta at the store.

I don't like to use the mix-and-extrude machines for fresh pasta; I prefer to make a dough and run it through a hand-crank machine such as the Atlas or Imperia. I never use semolina. Rather, I use all-purpose flour, or for a delicate pasta more like what I've had in Italy, I add a little pastry flour. The method for making this pasta follows.

I am not a gadget fan, but you should have a few essentials for making pasta. The dough can be made by hand or with a food processor. Purists will use a rolling pin to roll out sheets of dough, but a manual machine such as the Atlas or Imperia is useful. Motors can be added to these, but I have to say, I like the physical interaction I have with the kneading and rolling processes. Essential devices for cutting the pasta shapes include a fluted pastry wheel and biscuit cutters. The pasta makers have attachments for a variety of shapes. A large pot for cooking in ample water is a requirement. The ones with a strainer insert are nice, or you'll need a large strainer or colander. A drying rack is not essential, but it comes in handy if you are making a lot of pasta.

Fresh pasta isn't for every use. Heavy sauces require the strength of dried semolina pasta. The taste of dried pasta is unique; it is simply a different dish.

Pasta that has been properly dried can last a year on the shelf before it is cooked. Fresh pasta is only good for a few days in the refrigerator, depending upon the freshness of the eggs. It is better consumed when made.

Fresh pasta cooks quickly. Angel hair will only need thirty seconds to a minute; *fettuccine* will take a minute or two, and *ravioli* need two to three minutes. Dried pasta takes longer, as it needs to rehydrate. Pasta should not be soft or soggy when served. It should have a bite; the Italians call it *al dente,* "to the teeth." They believe that pasta cooked al dente is more easily digested and just tastes better. It is difficult to give an exact time, but in general, you should cook long, thin shapes like *fettuccine* or *spaghetti* for seven to eight minutes, and eight to ten minutes for short cuts like *penne.*

The best way to test for doneness is to bite into a sample. As you look at a cross section, you can see that the outer part (and the inner part of a hollow shape) cooks first; the color changes. The part that is uncooked in the center is still white. When that white is just about to disappear, the pasta is ready. The ambient heat will continue to cook it to just the right consistency by the time it is on the table. If you think you have overcooked the pasta, immediately add cold water to the pot to stop the cooking.

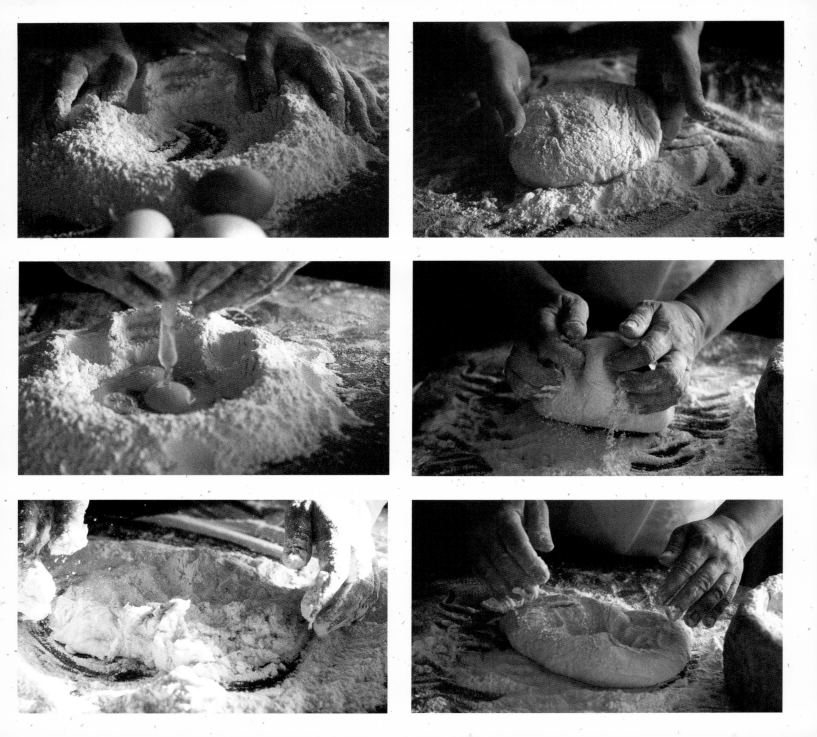

To determine quantities, allow approximately four ounces of dried pasta per person. The artisanally dried pasta will absorb more water when cooked, tripling the dry volume.

You must cook pasta in a large pot in plenty of water—at least six quarts for each pound of pasta being cooked. This is to keep the pasta from sticking together. Don't add oil. If the pasta has enough room to move around, and is stirred frequently while cooking, it won't stick. Before adding the pasta, liberally salt the water. This really adds to the flavor of the pasta. I use roughly two tablespoons of salt for each pound of pasta. Start with high heat to bring the water to a boil. Add the pasta a little at a time, stirring. As soon as the pasta is added, reduce the heat. Cook it, uncovered, stirring frequently with a wooden spoon to keep it from sticking. When you think the pasta is done to the right degree, drain it in a colander, reserving a little of the pasta-cooking water for your sauce, if needed.

Making Fresh Pasta

Makes just a little over 1 pound
2¹/₂ cups all-purpose flour
¹/₂ cup pastry flour
4 eggs (depending upon moisture needed)
1 tablespoon extra-virgin olive oil

MANUAL METHOD: Place the flours in a mound on a work surface. Make a well in the center and put in the eggs and oil. With your fingers, use a circular motion to gradually blend the egg mixture into the flour.

Gather the dough into a ball and knead by hand for 10 to 15 minutes, or until smooth and elastic. Set aside to rest for 15 minutes.

FOOD PROCESSOR METHOD: Place the flour in a food processor fitted with the steel knife blade.

In a small container with a pour spout, whisk the eggs with the oil.

With processor running, slowly add the egg mixture until the dough starts to come away from the sides of the bowl. Process for 30 seconds and check the consistency. The dough should be moist enough to pinch together, but not sticky.

On a lightly floured work surface, knead the dough to form a ball. Set aside to rest.

ADDING COLOR TO THE DOUGH: You can add color to the dough during the mixing process. It is easiest in the food processor. Add it to the flour and process well before adding any egg. Moist ingredients will cause you to add less egg. Green pasta dough can be derived by adding 3 ounces of spinach that has been steamed and squeezed very dry. A bunch of fresh basil gives a pastel green color and a wonderful aroma. A roasted and peeled red pepper turns the dough a lovely salmon color; a spoonful of tomato paste heads toward red. A teaspoon of cuttlefish, or squid, ink is the source of black pasta. A pinch of saffron in the eggs will give a sunny yellow color. Beets, carrots, even asparagus—any colorful vegetable—can be used as long as it is cooked well enough to purée to a smooth consistency.

ADDING FLAVOR TO THE DOUGH: The coloring ingredients add only a subtle flavor; they are primarily aesthetic. It is interesting to add spices and herbs for flavor—a tablespoon of coarsely ground black pepper or a teaspoon of minced fresh herbs, for example. For pasta to serve with seafood, a teaspoon of finely grated lemon zest is lovely. These ingredients all should be processed well with the flour before adding any egg.

ROLLING OUT THE DOUGH: Divide the dough into eight pieces and roll out one piece of the dough at a time. It should be thin enough that you can see your hand through it. Keep the remaining dough in a plastic bag to avoid drying it out.

With a rolling pin: Flatten the dough on a lightly floured work surface. Roll the dough, turning the disk to keep it even. Roll to desired thickness, let dry for 5 minutes on a lightly floured dish towel, then cut into desired pasta shape.

With a hand-cranked pasta maker: Start on the widest setting. Put the pasta through 8 to 10 times, folding it in half each time until the dough is smooth. If the dough tears, it may be too wet; dust it with flour, brushing off the excess.

Continue putting the dough through the rollers, without folding it, using a narrower setting each time until the dough is the desired thickness.

Allow the rolled dough to dry on a lightly floured dish towel while rolling the next piece of dough, then cut into desired pasta shape.

CUTTING THE DOUGH: The dough is ready to cut when it has dried slightly, but is still tender and flexible. It feels like soft suede.

By hand: For long shapes such as *pappardelle, fettuccine,* or *linguine,* gently fold the sheet of pasta several times. With a sharp knife, cut across the folds to the desired width.

To make fresh *garganelli,* as shown below, cut 2-inch squares of fresh pasta dough. Press each square on a wooden pasta comb with your hand or a small rolling pin to get the striations on the outside. Wrap the striated squares around a 1/2-inch-thick wooden dowel or pencil, starting with one corner and rolling to the other. Seal corners with a little water or egg wash.

By machine: The manual machines have attachments for each shape. Simply crank a sheet of pasta through using the appropriate attachment.

NOTE: After being cut, let the pasta rest on a lightly floured dish towel until ready to cook. Long pasta, especially if the dough was moist, should be fluffed occasionally to keep it from sticking.

STUFFING THE PASTA: When making stamped or straight-sided shapes such as *ravioli,* place a sheet of pasta on a lightly floured work surface. Spoon the filling on the pasta at regular intervals. Lightly brush the exposed surface with an egg wash or water. Top with a second sheet of pasta and press with your fingers along the edges and around each mound of filling to seal. Cut the desired shape with a knife or pastry wheel.

To make circular or folded shapes such as *tortellini,* first cut the shape with a biscuit cutter. Place a small amount of filling in the center; be sure the edges are clean so the seal will be secure. Lightly brush the exposed surface with an egg wash or water and fold, pressing tightly to seal.

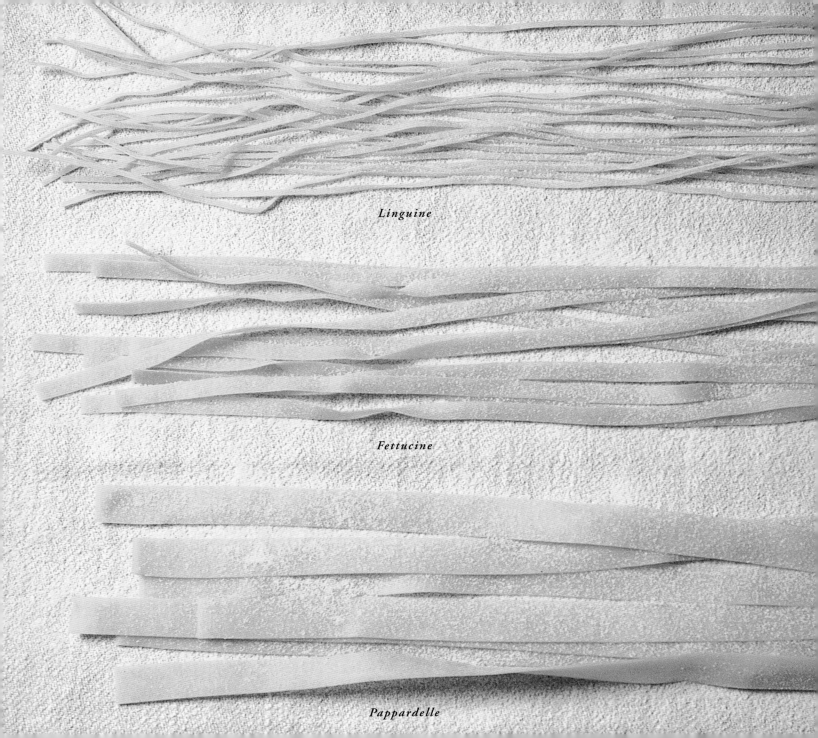

Linguine

Fettucine

Pappardelle

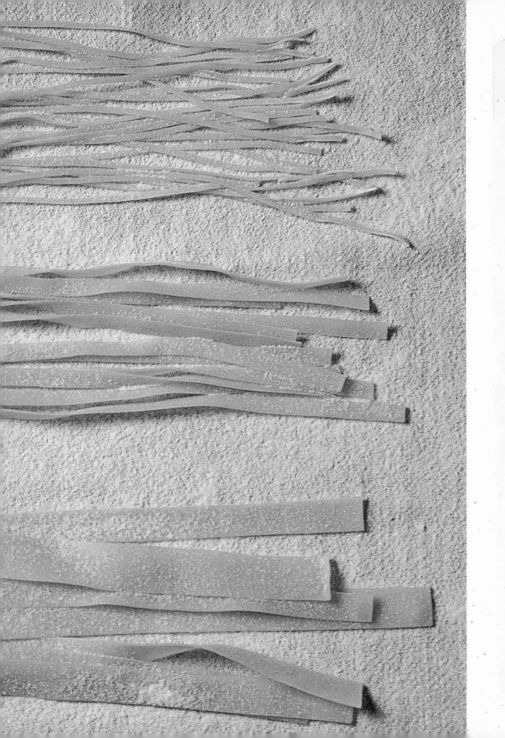

The North

"No man is lonely while eating spaghetti."

ROBERT MORLEY

Tagliolini con Ragù di Fegatini

Tagliolini with Chicken Liver Sauce

The name tagliolini means "cut finely." These noodles should be about 1/8 inch wide.
This dish is delicious made with dried pasta as well.

3 tablespoons unsalted butter

¹/4 cup minced onion

8 ounces chicken livers, cleaned and coarsely chopped

2 cups chicken stock (page 106), heated

Sea salt and freshly ground black pepper

Fresh Pasta Dough (page 31), rolled and

cut into tagliolini

2 tablespoons minced flat-leaf parsley

In a sauté pan, heat the butter over medium heat. Add the onion and chicken livers and cook for 3 to 4 minutes, until the onion has softened and the liver is firm. Add the stock and cook for 6 to 8 minutes longer, until the liver is tender and the sauce has slightly thickened. Season with salt and pepper to taste.

In a large pot of salted boiling water, cook the pasta 2 to 3 minutes, until al dente. Drain, turn into a warmed serving bowl, and toss with the sauce. Garnish with parsley and serve at once. *Serves 6*

Tajarin con la Fonduta

Tagliolini with Fontina Sauce

Tajarin is the local dialect for tagliolini, a classic Piemontese pasta. In the fall it is often found with this classic sauce and garnished with paper-thin slices of fresh white truffle. A half teaspoon of truffle oil can be added.

12 ounces fontina cheese, coarsely grated

1 cup milk, warmed

¼ cup unsalted butter

3 egg yolks, lightly beaten

Sea salt and freshly ground black pepper

Fresh Pasta Dough (page 31), rolled and

cut crosswise very fine

In a mixing bowl, combine the cheese and milk. Let stand for 30 minutes.

In a heavy-bottomed saucepan over low heat (or in the top of a double boiler), melt the butter. Add the cheese-milk mixture, whisking, until the cheese has melted. Transfer the mixture to a blender and add the egg yolks slowly. Season with salt and pepper and return to the saucepan. Keep warm over very low heat, stirring occasionally.

In a large pot of salted boiling water, cook the pasta for about 2 minutes, until al dente. Drain, turn into a warmed serving bowl, and toss with the sauce. Serve at once. *Serves 4*

Agnolotti al Tartufo

Pasta with Truffles

Since most of us don't have white truffles handy, I am suggesting truffle oil in this recipe. Look for an oil that lists truffle among its ingredients, preferably with tiny bits of truffle in the bottle. If you do have a white truffle (lucky you!), use it as a condiment, shaved over the dish just as it is served.

3 tablespoons extra-virgin olive oil

1/4 cup minced onion

1/4 pound lean ground pork

1/4 pound ground veal

2 ounces prosciutto di Parma, minced

3/4 cup freshly grated
Parmigiano-Reggiano cheese

3 eggs

1/2 teaspoon truffle oil

Sea salt and freshly ground black pepper

Fresh Pasta Dough (page 31), rolled and
cut into 4-inch circles

6 tablespoons unsalted butter

Tartufo bianco d'Alba (fresh white truffle)

In a sauté pan over medium heat, heat the olive oil. Add the onion, ground meats, and prosciutto and cook 4 to 5 minutes, until the meat is no longer pink. Remove with a slotted spoon to a bowl to cool. When cooled, add 1/4 cup of the Parmigiano-Reggiano, 2 eggs, and truffle oil. Season with salt and pepper.

Beat the remaining egg with a teaspoon of water for the egg wash. Place a teaspoonful of filling in the center of each pasta circle. Brush the edges with the egg wash and fold the circle in half, sealing the edges well. Set aside on a lightly floured dish towel until ready to cook.

In a small saucepan, melt the unsalted butter until foaming. Keep warm.

In a large pot of salted boiling water, cook the agnolotti for 3 to 4 minutes, until al dente. Drain, turn into a warmed serving bowl, and toss with the melted butter. Sprinkle with the remaining 1/2 cup Parmigiano-Reggiano. Using a truffle slicer or mandoline, shave thin slices of the white truffle over the pasta to cover. Serve at once. *Serves 4*

Bìgoli in Salsa

Whole-Wheat Spaghetti in Anchovy Sauce with Radicchio

If you have a bìgolaro, a simple Venetian extrusion device, you can make a fresh dough using 2 cups whole-wheat flour, 2 eggs, and a pinch of salt (follow instructions on page 31). Otherwise, roll out the dough and cut by a standard method into spaghetti. You can also substitute dried whole-wheat spaghetti.

¹/₄ cup extra-virgin olive oil

¹/₄ cup minced onion

8 ounces anchovy fillets (packed in oil)

1 cup dry white wine

Freshly ground pepper

1 pound bìgoli

¹/₄ cup minced flat-leaf parsley, for garnish

In a saucepan, heat the oil over medium heat. Add the onion and anchovies (reserving 6 small pieces for garnish), cover, and simmer for 10 minutes. Deglaze the pan with the wine, stirring to loosen any cooked particles from the pan. Continue to simmer for 20 minutes longer, until the anchovies are falling apart and the sauce is creamy. Season with pepper.

In a large pot of salted boiling water, cook the pasta according to package directions, until al dente. Drain, turn into a warmed serving bowl, and toss with the sauce. Garnish with the reserved anchovy and parsley and serve at once.

Serves 6

Linguine ai Quattro Formaggi

Linguine with Four Cheeses

Any combination of soft cheeses will work well in this sauce. Short tube pastas are a nice substitution as they allow the wonderful sauce to be carried inside and out.

1/2 cup heavy cream

2 ounces fontina cheese, grated

2 ounces Gorgonzola cheese, crumbled

2 ounces mozzarella cheese, grated

1/2 teaspoon minced fresh thyme

Sea salt and freshly ground black pepper

1 pound linguine

1/4 cup freshly grated Parmigiano-Reggiano cheese

In a saucepan, combine the cream, fontina, Gorgonzola, and mozzarella. Warm slowly over low heat, stirring constantly, until cheeses have melted. Add the thyme, season with salt and pepper, set aside, and keep warm.

In a large pot of salted boiling water, cook the pasta according to package directions, until al dente. Drain and transfer to a warm platter. Spoon the cheese sauce over the top, sprinkle with the Parmigiano-Reggiano, and serve at once. *Serves 4*

Penne Rigati al Gorgonzola

Penne Rigati with Gorgonzola Sauce

This rich dish is delicious served with sautéed medallions of lamb. Gorgonzola dolce latte is a milder, sweeter version of Lombardy's blue cheese, but the base of this sauce also works well with goat cheese.

1 pound penne rigati, or other short tube pasta

Olive oil for tossing pasta

2 cloves garlic, minced

1 shallot, minced

1 cup dry white wine

2 cups heavy cream

4 ounces Gorgonzola dolce latte, crumbled

1 tablespoon fresh thyme, minced

Sea salt and freshly ground white pepper to taste

In a large pot of salted boiling water, cook the pasta according to package directions, until al dente. Drain and reserve 1 cup of the pasta-cooking liquid. Toss the pasta with a little olive oil and set aside in a warm place.

Place garlic, shallot, and wine in sauté pan and reduce to a thick glaze. Add the cream and reduce slightly. Lower heat to a simmer and add the gorgonzola, stirring until melted. Season with thyme, salt, and pepper. Toss with pasta and serve at once. *Serves 4*

Pizzoccheri della Valtellina

Buckwheat Pasta with Vegetables

This recipe is from the valley of Teglio in northern Italy, near the Alps. The heartiness of this nutty brown pasta sustains mountain life, especially that of skiers in the winter.

2 cups fine buckwheat flour

1 cup unbleached all-purpose flour

1 egg

2/3 cup milk

2 potatoes, peeled and sliced 1/4 inch thick

1 head savoy cabbage, julienned

4 ounces Taleggio cheese, sliced

Sea salt and freshly ground black pepper

3 tablespoons unsalted butter

6 sage leaves

In a large mixing bowl, combine the flours. Add the egg and milk and mix well, turning onto a lightly floured work surface to knead when it becomes too stiff to stir. With a rolling pin or pasta maker, roll the dough into thin sheets (see method, page 32). Cut the noodles to 1/2 inch by 2 inches. Set aside on a lightly floured dish towel to dry until ready to cook.

In a large pot of boiling salted water, cook the potatoes and cabbage for 8 to 10 minutes, until the potatoes are tender, but firm. Remove the vegetables with a slotted spoon and set aside. Return the water to a boil and add the pasta. Cook for 2 to 3 minutes, until al dente. Drain.

Preheat an oven to 400°. In a lightly buttered casserole dish, layer the pasta pieces with the vegetables and cheese. Season with salt and pepper to taste. Place in the oven for 10 minutes to melt the cheese.

Meanwhile, in a sauté pan, heat the butter over medium heat until foaming. Add the sage leaves and sauté them until softened. Pour over the top of the casserole and serve at once.

Serves 6

Raviolo di Maiale con Mostarda

Raviolo of Pork with Mostarda

These large ravioli make a sumptuous first course when served singly.
Mostarda is a mixture of candied fruits preserved in a liquid of sugar and mustard-flavored oil. You can find
it in gourmet Italian food stores packed in jars or beautifully decorated tins.

FILLING

3 tablespoons extra-virgin olive oil

1 cup diced red onion

12 ounces boneless pork loin, cut into 1/2-inch cubes

1 teaspoon freshly grated orange zest, plus

6 strips for garnish

1/4 cup good-quality balsamic vinegar

1 potato, diced into 1/2-inch cubes and

cooked until tender

3 tablespoons water

Sea salt and freshly ground black pepper

Fresh Pasta Dough (page 31), rolled and cut into

5-inch squares with a fluted pastry wheel

1 egg, beaten, with 1 teaspoon water for egg wash

6 tablespoons mostarda

To make the filling: Heat the olive oil in a medium sauté pan over medium heat. Add the onion and cook until softened, but not browned. Add the pork and orange zest and cook for 6 to 8 minutes longer, until browned. Deglaze the pan with the balsamic vinegar, stirring to loosen any browned bits from the pan. Add the potatoes and water and cook until reduced, about 3 to 4 minutes. Season with salt and pepper; remove from the heat.

To assemble the ravioli: Place 2 heaping tablespoons of the cooled filling on 6 of the pasta squares. Brush the edges with egg wash and top with another pasta square, pressing the edges firmly to seal.

In a large pot of salted boiling water, cook the ravioli for 3 to 4 minutes, until al dente. Drain and place on individual serving plates. With a very sharp knife, make a slit in the top to expose the filling. Top with a tablespoon of mostarda, garnish with an orange strip, and serve at once. *Serves 6*

Lasagna Bolognese

Meaty Lasagna

This is a classic pasta dish in Bologna, truly the heartland of fresh pasta. Spend a day roaming the market streets just off Piazza Maggiore, and you will understand the passion the Bolognese feel for food. My favorite shop is Tamburini, a gastronomic paradise located at Via Caprarie, 1.

MEAT SAUCE

1/4 cup extra-virgin olive oil

2 medium onions, diced

1 stalk celery, diced

1 carrot, peeled and diced

1 clove garlic, minced

1 pound ground beef

1 pound ground lean pork

1 cup cream

1 cup red wine

2 cups veal stock (page 107)

2 pounds ripe tomatoes, peeled (page 107) and coarsely chopped

1 sprig of rosemary

1 sprig of flat-leaf parsley

1 sprig of thyme

Sea salt and freshly ground black pepper

Fresh Pasta Dough (page 31), made with spinach variation and rolled into sheets

BALSAMELLA

1 quart milk

6 tablespoons butter

1/3 cup flour

Sea salt and freshly ground white pepper

Freshly ground nutmeg

1/2 pound fresh mozzarella cheese, cut into 1/4-inch-thick slices

1 bunch basil, julienned

1 pound plum tomatoes, cut into 1/4-inch-thick slices

1/2 cup freshly grated Parmigiano-Reggiano cheese

To make the meat sauce: In a large skillet, heat the oil over medium heat and add the onion, celery, and carrot. Cook until golden brown, about 5 to 7 minutes. Add the garlic and the meats and cook, stirring constantly, until browned. Add the cream and reduce until thickened, about 6 to 8 minutes. Add the wine and reduce until thickened, about 6 to 8 minutes. Add the veal stock, chopped tomatoes, and herbs. Let simmer for 1 to 1 1/2 hours, stirring occasionally, until thickened. Remove and discard the herb sprigs. Season with salt and pepper. Set aside to cool.

Cut the fresh pasta into strips to fit baking dish. Set aside on a lightly floured work surface to dry.

To make the balsamella: In a medium saucepan over medium heat, heat the milk to scalding. In another saucepan, over medium heat, melt the butter. Whisk in the flour and cook for 1 to 2 minutes, until foamy. Whisk in the hot milk and return to a medium heat. Cook, whisking constantly until thickened. Season with salt, pepper, and nutmeg.

Preheat the oven to 350°. Lightly oil a 13 by 9-inch baking dish.

In a large pot of salted boiling water, cook the pasta until al dente, about 3 minutes. Drain and set aside in a bowl of cool water until ready to assemble lasagna.

Spoon a coating of balsamella in the bottom of the prepared baking dish. Assemble the lasagna in layers, starting with a layer of pasta. Top with half of the meat sauce, spreading evenly, followed by a layer of mozzarella cheese, a sprinkling of basil, then a layer of sliced tomatoes. Repeat, finishing with pasta. Cover the top with the balsamella, sprinkle with the Parmigiano-Reggiano, and bake for 30 to 40 minutes, until lightly browned. Serve at once. *Serves 8*

Garganelli agli Asparagi

Garganelli with Asparagus

In the spring, this is delightful with asparagi selvatica, wispy wild asparagus.
This recipe calls for dried garganelli, or the short dried pasta of your choice. To make fresh garganelli,
see the instructions and photo on page 32.

1/2 cup butter

1 pound asparagus, blanched and

cut into 3-inch-long pieces

1/2 teaspoon salt

1 teaspoon freshly ground black pepper

1 pound garganelli

1/2 cup freshly grated

Parmigiano-Reggiano cheese

In a large skillet, melt the butter over low heat. Add the asparagus and toss to coat. Season with salt and pepper and set aside.

In a large pot of salted boiling water, cook the pasta according to package directions, until al dente. Drain, toss with the asparagus and Parmigiano-Reggiano. Turn into a warmed serving bowl and serve at once. *Serves 6*

Tagliatelle alla Bolognese

Tagliatelle with Meat Sauce

*Tagliatelle are about 3/8-inch-wide ribbons, but any fresh pasta shape
will transport you to Bologna with this classic sauce. You can also use a pound of dried pasta.
Ground meats can also be used in place of the chopped meats.*

1/4 cup extra-virgin olive oil

1/4 pound pancetta, very finely minced

1 onion, minced

1 stalk celery, minced

1 carrot, minced

1/2 pound veal, very finely minced

1/4 pound pork, very finely minced

1 cup veal stock (page 107)

1 (12-ounce) can of whole peeled tomatoes

1/4 cup heavy cream

Sea salt and freshly ground black pepper

Freshly ground nutmeg

Fresh Pasta Dough (page 31), rolled and
cut into tagliatelle

In a large saucepan, heat the oil over medium-high heat. Add the pancetta, onion, celery, and carrot and sauté for 4 to 5 minutes, or until golden.

Add the chopped meats and cook until browned. Add the stock and the tomatoes. Simmer, stirring frequently, for 35 to 40 minutes, or until thickened. Stir in the cream and heat through. Season to taste with salt, pepper, and nutmeg.

In a large pot of salted boiling water, cook the pasta 2 to 3 minutes, until al dente. Drain and turn into a warmed serving bowl, spoon the sauce over the top, and serve at once.

Serves 6

Gramigna con Burro Fuso

Gramigna with Sage-Infused Butter Sauce

*Gramigna literally means "weed," which is what these short strands look like.
As the short, fresh noodles dry, they curl a little, giving a "weedy" effect. Dried spaghetti or bucatini
can be substituted; break the noodles into 3-inch lengths before cooking.*

*Fresh Pasta Dough (page 31), rolled and
cut into spaghetti-sized strands*
¹/4 cup unsalted butter
24 small fresh sage leaves
³/4 cup freshly grated Parmigiano-Reggiano cheese

Cut the pasta strands into 3-inch lengths and place on a lightly floured work surface to dry for 30 minutes.

In a saucepan, melt the butter. Add the sage leaves and simmer for 5 minutes. Remove from the heat and keep warm.

In a large pot of salted boiling water, cook the pasta 2 to 3 minutes, until al dente. Drain and turn into a warmed serving bowl, spoon the sauce over the top, sprinkle with the cheese, and serve at once. *Serves 6*

Farfalle con Piselli e Prosciutto

Farfalle with Peas and Prosciutto

Farfalle, or butterfly pasta, is found in many regions from north to south.
Here it is paired with peas, cream, and prosciutto di Parma, the salty, sweet cured meat
from Emilia-Romagna, to create a northern Italian classic.

4 tablespoons unsalted butter

1 small spring onion, sliced

1 cup heavy cream

2 cups shelled spring peas

Sea salt and freshly ground white pepper

1 pound farfalle or pasta of your choice

1/4 pound thinly sliced prosciutto di Parma,
cut into thin strips

Freshly grated Parmigiano-Reggiano cheese

In a sauté pan over medium heat, melt the butter. Add the onion and sauté until softened, but not browned. Add the cream and heat through. Stir in the peas and simmer for 3 to 5 minutes, until the peas are tender. Season with salt and pepper and keep warm.

In a large pot of salted boiling water, cook the pasta according to package directions, until al dente. Drain and toss with the sauce. Transfer to a warmed serving platter, garnish with the prosciutto, and serve with Parmigiano-Reggiano on the side. *Serves 4*

Tortellini con Burro e Formaggio

Tortellini with Butter and Cheese

Stories abound detailing the origin of this famous pasta. My favorite is the innkeeper/chef who was inspired to invent the dish after peering through a keyhole at a beautiful lady bathing. The sight of her navel in the bathwater led to the creation of an umbilically shaped delicacy we know as tortellini.

2 ounces prosciutto di Parma

1/4 pound ground veal

1 cup freshly grated Parmigiano-Reggiano

Fresh Pasta Dough (page 31), rolled into sheets

1 egg, beaten, with 1 teaspoon water for egg wash

1/2 cup unsalted butter, melted

Grind prosciutto di Parma in the food processor. Stir in the ground veal and 1/2 cup Parmigiano-Reggiano by hand. Place in a piping bag and set aside.

Cut the pasta into 2-inch rounds. Pipe approximately 1/2 teaspoon filling in the center of each round, brush the edges with egg wash, and fold in half to form a half-moon shape. Wrap it around your finger, bringing the corners together to overlap, pinching tightly to seal the shape into a circle. Curl the thin edges of the pasta back. Set aside on a lightly floured surface.

In a large pot of salted boiling water, cook the tortellini for 3 to 5 minutes, until al dente. Drain the tortellini, toss them with the melted butter and the remaining 1/2 cup Parmigiano-Reggiano. Transfer to a warmed serving dish and serve at once. *Serves 6*

Tortellini

Tortelloni

Ravioli

Central Italy

"Life is a combination of magic and pasta."

FEDERICO FELLINI

Trofie al Pesto

Pasta with Pesto

Trofie is a pasta most often found with pesto, along the coast of Liguria. To make it by hand, knead together 2 cups all-purpose flour, 1/2 teaspoon sea salt, and 3/4 to 1 cup of boiling water to a smooth consistency. Tear off penny-sized pieces and roll them under your palm until about 1 inch long with thin ends.

PESTO SAUCE

3 cloves garlic, peeled

1 bunch fresh basil, stemmed

1/4 cup pine nuts, toasted (page 107)

1/2 cup extra-virgin olive oil

1/4 cup finely grated Parmigiano-Reggiano cheese

1 pound fresh or dried trofie, or pasta of your choice

2 medium potatoes, peeled and sliced 1/2 inch thick and blanched for 4 minutes (page 107)

1/2 pound green beans, cut into 3-inch lengths and blanched for 4 minutes (page 107)

To make the pesto: With a food processor running, drop in the garlic. Add the basil and pine nuts and process to a grainy texture. With the machine running, gradually add the olive oil to the desired consistency. Fold in the cheese by hand. Set the pesto aside.

In a large pot of salted boiling water, cook the pasta according to package directions, until al dente. Add the potatoes and green beans for the last minute of cooking to warm them. Drain, reserving 1 cup of the pasta-cooking liquid.

Toss the pesto with the pasta, adding the pasta-cooking liquid to the desired consistency. Turn into a warmed serving bowl and serve at once. *Serves 6*

Corzetti di Liguria

Stamped Pasta

Corzetti are little disks of dough that have an impression pressed into them. The pattern is sometimes symbolic, geometric, iconic, or it may even be the producer's initials. The indentations provide a texture that helps hold the sauce. To achieve a colorful dish, you need to make two or three doughs (see page 31), but it would taste just as delicious if the disks were all the same color.

WHITE CORZETTI

1 1/4 cups unbleached all-purpose flour

1 egg, beaten with 1 tablespoon water

ORANGE CORZETTI

1 1/4 cups unbleached all-purpose flour

1 egg, beaten with 2 tablespoons tomato purée

SAUCE

1/2 cup unsalted butter, melted

1/2 cup freshly grated Parmigiano-Reggiano cheese

1/4 cup julienned fresh basil

1/4 cup pine nuts, toasted (see page 107)

To make the corzetti: Make each different colored dough separately. Place the flour in a mixing bowl. Add the egg-water mixture, or the egg-tomato mixture for the orange corzetti, and stir until moistened. On a lightly floured work surface, knead the dough to form a smooth ball. Place the dough in a plastic bag to rest for 15 minutes.

Roll out the pasta as directed on page 32. Allow the rolled dough to dry on a lightly floured work surface while rolling the next piece of dough.

Using a 3-inch round cookie cutter, cut the dough into circles. Stamp with a corzetti stamp (see Resources, page 108), or make a crosshatch with the tines of a fork.

In a large pot of salted boiling water, cook the corzetti for about 2 minutes, until al dente. Drain and toss gently with the butter, Parmigiano-Reggiano, basil, and pine nuts. Transfer to a warm serving platter and serve at once. *Serves 6*

Trenette col Tocco du Noxe

Pasta with Walnut Sauce

Liguria's long coast made it an early port to receive trade from the south. The tradition of pasta here is a long one. The region has a superior microclimate that is very conducive to growing early vegetables and herbs. Tocco du noxe is dialect for a "touch of walnuts," an apt description for this creamy pesto.

2 cloves garlic

¹/₄ pound walnuts, toasted (page 107)

¹/₃ cup extra-virgin olive oil

1 slice of country bread, soaked in ¹/₃ cup milk

¹/₄ cup freshly grated Parmigiano-Reggiano cheese

Sea salt and freshly ground white pepper

Fresh Pasta Dough (page 31), rolled and cut into ¹/₁₆-inch-wide noodles

Flat-leaf parsley leaves, for garnish

In a food processor, with the motor running, drop in the garlic to mince. Add the walnuts (reserve 2 tablespoons for garnish), olive oil, and the bread-milk mixture. Process until smooth. Fold in the Parmigiano-Reggiano by hand. Season with salt and pepper.

In a large pot of salted boiling water, cook the pasta for 2 to 3 minutes, until al dente. Drain, reserving 1 cup of the pasta-cooking liquid. Toss the walnut pesto with the pasta, adding the pasta-cooking liquid to the desired consistency. Turn into a warmed serving bowl, sprinkle with reserved walnuts and parsley, and serve at once. *Serves 6*

Spaghetti alla Norcina con Tartufo Nero

Spaghetti with Pork and Black Truffle

This recipe is incredible with fresh truffle and is also good without it. If you don't want to do without the taste of truffle, the options include flash frozen—probably the best substitute—or truffles preserved in water and salt and packed in jars or tins. There are also truffle oils, pastes, creams, and powders. Look for a product that lists truffle among its ingredients, and substitute it to your taste.

3 tablespoons extra-virgin olive oil

1/2 cup diced onion

12 ounces boneless pork loin, cut into 1/2-inch cubes

1/4 cup red wine

3 cups veal stock (page 107)

1 fresh truffle, sliced paper-thin

Sea salt and freshly ground black pepper

1 pound spaghetti

Heat the olive oil in a medium sauté pan over medium heat. Add the onion and cook until softened, but not browned. Add the pork and cook for 6 to 8 minutes longer, until browned. Deglaze the pan with the wine, stirring to loosen the browned bits from the surface of the pan. Cook until reduced by half. Add the veal stock and simmer for 20 to 30 minutes, until the pork is very tender. Add the truffle, season with salt and pepper, and keep warm.

In a large pot of salted boiling water, cook the pasta according to package directions, until al dente. Drain and toss with the sauce. Transfer to a warmed serving bowl and serve at once. *Serves 6*

Gnocchi con Pomodori

Potato Gnocchi with Oven-Roasted Tomatoes

Gnocchi is one of those cross-regional pasta shapes. The recipe can vary from region to region, but this version is the one generally found. Pesto sauce (page 59) is also very good with gnocchi.

2 large (about 1 3/4 pounds) baking potatoes, peeled and boiled until tender

1 2/3 cups unbleached all-purpose flour

2 eggs

6 large ripe tomatoes, cored and cut into wedges

1/4 cup extra-virgin olive oil

Sea salt and freshly ground black pepper

8 ounces fresh mozzarella, cut into 1/4-inch cubes

1/4 cup julienned fresh basil, for garnish

Preheat an oven to 425°.

While the potatoes are still warm, put them through a ricer or food mill. Place the potatoes in a large mixing bowl and let cool. Add the flour and eggs and mix until well combined. Turn onto a well-floured work surface and knead until soft and smooth. Divide into 8 pieces and roll each into a long rope, about 1/2 inch in diameter. Cut into 1-inch lengths. Press with tines of a fork or roll gently against a nutmeg grater to give the outside some texture. Set aside on a floured surface until ready to cook.

Toss the tomato wedges with olive oil. Season with salt and pepper. Place in a single layer in a baking dish. Roast in the oven until the tomato skins have lightly browned, about 15 minutes.

In a large pot of salted boiling water, cook the gnocchi for 6 to 8 minutes, until they rise to the surface. Drain and turn into a warmed serving bowl. Toss with the roasted tomato and mozzarella. Garnish with basil and serve at once.

Serves 6

Ravioli Patate de Mugello

Ravioli Filled with Potato from the Mugello

The first time I enjoyed these silky delights was at the home of Anna Mignani,
the owner of Casa di Caccia, a hunting lodge in the hills northeast of Florence called the Mugello.
Serve these with a simple sage and butter sauce (page 51) or one of the meat ragù sauces.

1/4 cup extra-virgin olive oil

1/2 stalk celery, very finely minced

2 tablespoons very finely minced carrot

2 tablespoons very finely minced onion

1/2 cup dry white wine

2 cups chicken stock (page 106)

1 cup diced potatoes (about 1/2 large potato)

1/4 cup freshly grated Parmigiano-Reggiano cheese

2 eggs, plus 1 egg beaten with 1 teaspoon water
for egg wash

Sea salt and freshly ground black pepper

Fresh Pasta Dough (page 31), rolled into sheets

In a sauté pan, over medium-high heat, heat the olive oil. Sauté the celery, carrot, and onion until golden brown, about 5 to 6 minutes. Deglaze the pan with the wine, stirring to loosen any cooked particles from the pan. Reduce over high heat 3 to 4 minutes, until thickened. Add the stock and bring to a boil. Add the potatoes and cook over medium heat for 20 to 25 minutes, until the vegetables are very tender and the sauce has thickened. Pass the mixture through a ricer or a food mill.

When cooled, fold in the Parmigiano-Reggiano and 2 eggs. Season with salt and pepper.

Place a sheet of pasta on a lightly floured work surface. Place 1/2 teaspoon of filling every 3 inches down the length of one side of the pasta sheet. Lightly brush the other side of the sheet with the egg wash. Fold the sheet in half lengthwise and press with your fingers along the edges to seal. Cut around each lump of filling with a pastry wheel into half moon shapes. Set aside on a lightly floured dish towel until ready to cook.

In a large pot of salted boiling water, cook the pasta for about 2 minutes, until al dente. Serve with the sauce of choice. *Serves 6 (makes about 6 dozen ravioli)*

Capellini Vongole

Angel-Hair Pasta with Clams

*"Lucky Napoléon" wrote Dylan Thomas to friends in 1947. The island of Elba
is where Napoleon was exiled in the early 1800s. It is worth the trip by ferry from the mainland
of Tuscany, if only to enjoy the spectacular seafood, caught fresh daily.*

2 dozen fresh clams

$1/2$ cup dry white wine

$1/2$ cup water

Sprig of fresh rosemary, plus

1 teaspoon rosemary, minced

8 cloves garlic

1 small onion, diced

1 large carrot, peeled and diced

1 stalk celery, diced

2 ripe tomatoes, peeled (page 107) and seeded

1 tablespoon fresh thyme, minced

2 tablespoons fresh parsley, minced

Sea salt and freshly ground black pepper

1 pound angel-hair pasta

Scrub the clams with a brush, rinsing well to remove sand from the shell. Place in a large pot with wine, water, and the sprig of rosemary. Cover and steam over low heat for about 15 minutes, until the clams pop open. Discard any that don't open. Remove with slotted spoon to cool. Strain the broth and return it to the pot.

Bring the broth to a boil and add garlic, onion, carrot, celery, and tomato. Reduce to medium heat, reducing the broth and cooking until the vegetables are tender, about 10 minutes. Add the thyme, parsley, minced rosemary, and salt and pepper to taste. Just before serving, add the clams back to the sauce; allow to reheat, but don't overcook them.

In a large pot of salted boiling water, cook the pasta according to package directions, until al dente. Drain and transfer to a warm platter. Ladle the clams and their sauce over the top and serve at once. *Serves 6*

Pici all' Aglione

Pasta with Garlic Tomato Sauce

I learned how to make hand-rolled pici, a pasta found only in a small area of southern Tuscany, from Massimiliano Mariotti, chef at Al Casale in Chianciano Terme. Although it is possible to buy dried products called pici, it should only be called pici when it is fresh. When dry, it is called spaghettone, or fat spaghetti. Aglione is a type of wild garlic, similar to green, or immature, garlic. You can substitute mature garlic but use half the amount.

4 cups unbleached all-purpose flour

1 1/4 cups water

3 tablespoons extra-virgin olive oil

Pinch of salt

6 large, very ripe tomatoes, peeled (page 107), seeded, and coarsely chopped

1 small head green garlic (approximately 6 immature cloves), sliced

1 or 2 peperoncini (dry red chiles) to taste

1/4 cup finely chopped flat-leaf parsley

Sea salt and freshly ground black pepper

On a wooden board, make a well in the flour. Add the water, 1 tablespoon olive oil, and salt. With your hands, work the flour into the liquid and work the dough to a smooth and homogenous texture. Cut the dough in small pieces and roll with the palm of your hand into a long, round string; this technique is actually called *piciare*. The thinner the pici, the better.

In a large saucepan, combine the tomatoes, garlic, the remaining olive oil, peperoncini, and parsley. Over medium heat, simmer for 30 to 35 minutes, stirring occasionally, until the garlic is very tender (mature garlic will take longer). Season with salt and pepper to taste. Keep warm.

In a large pot of salted boiling water, cook the pasta 6 to 8 minutes, until al dente. Toss with the sauce, turn into a warmed serving bowl, and serve at once. *Serves 6*

Pappardelle con Ragù di Cinghiale

Pasta with Wild Boar Sauce

Tuscany in the fall means wild boar. A long-simmered ragù is the perfect cold weather food. I have listed a resource for boar (page 108), but it is quite tasty to substitute pork.

1/4 cup extra-virgin olive oil plus extra for tossing pasta

1 onion, very finely minced

1 stalk celery, very finely minced

2 carrots, peeled and very finely minced

2 cloves garlic

1 1/2 pounds boneless wild boar leg meat, coarsely chopped

2 cups red wine

6 large ripe tomatoes, peeled (page 107), seeded, and diced

1 tablespoon juniper berries

1 sprig of rosemary

Sea salt and freshly ground black pepper

24 ounces dried pappardelle, or

Fresh Pasta Dough (page 31), rolled and cut into 1/2-inch-wide strands

In a sauté pan over medium-high heat, heat the olive oil. Sauté the vegetables until golden brown, about 5 to 6 minutes. Add the chopped meat and cook until browned, about 3 to 4 minutes. Add the red wine and cook until thickened.

Add the tomato, juniper berries, and rosemary. Simmer, uncovered, over a low flame, stirring occasionally, for 35 to 40 minutes, until meat is tender and the sauce has thickened. Season with salt and pepper to taste.

In a large pot of salted boiling water, cook the dried pasta according to package directions, or the fresh pasta 3 minutes, until al dente. Drain and toss with olive oil. Turn into a warmed serving bowl, spoon the sauce on top, and serve at once. *Serves 8*

Penne Primavera

Pasta with Fava Beans and Spring Vegetables

Don't feel constrained by the ingredients listed here—use your favorite pasta,
along with the best seasonal vegetables.

1 pound penne, or pasta of your choice

2 pounds fresh fava beans, podded and
blanched 1 minute (page 107)

1/4 cup extra-virgin olive oil plus extra for tossing pasta

1 red spring onion, peeled and diced

1 bunch baby carrots, peeled, cut in half lengthwise, and
blanched 2 minutes

Sea salt and freshly ground black pepper

1/2 cup freshly grated Parmigiano-Reggiano cheese

6 zucchini flowers, cleaned and blanched 30 seconds

In a large pot of salted boiling water, cook the pasta according to package directions, until al dente. Drain and reserve 1 cup of the pasta-cooking liquid. Toss the pasta with a little of the olive oil and set aside in a warm place.

Remove the outer shell from two-thirds of the largest fava beans by pinching off the end and squeezing the brightly colored bean out. Leave about one-third of the smallest beans in their outer shell.

In a large sauté pan, heat the oil and sauté the onion for 3 to 4 minutes, or until golden brown. Add 1 cup of the pasta-cooking liquid and bring to a boil. Reduce over high heat by one-half, then lower the heat to a simmer; add the carrots and the peeled and unpeeled fava beans. Heat 3 to 4 minutes, until vegetables are warmed through. Season with salt and pepper.

Toss the vegetable mixture with the pasta and turn into a warmed serving bowl. Stir in the Parmigiano-Reggiano, garnish with the zucchini flowers, and serve at once. *Serves 6*

Malfatti con Rucola e Pancetta

Pasta with Arugula and Pancetta

In the fall, this dish is made with cavolo nero, or Tuscan kale. Arugula is a delicious spicy substitute that makes a quick summer dish.

Approximately 4 cups leftover scraps from making fresh pasta shapes

1/4 cup extra-virgin olive oil plus extra for tossing pasta

4 ounces pancetta, diced

1 medium onion, diced

3 cups arugula

Sea salt and freshly ground black pepper

In a large pot of salted boiling water, cook the pasta pieces 3 to 4 minutes, until al dente. Drain and toss with olive oil. Keep warm.

In a sauté pan, over medium-high heat, heat the 1/4 cup olive oil. Sauté the pancetta and onion until golden brown, about 5 to 6 minutes. Add the arugula, stirring just to wilt slightly. Season with salt and pepper and toss immediately with the pasta. Serve at once. *Serves 4*

Farro con Ricotta e Verdure

Farro Pasta with Ricotta and Grilled Vegetables

Farro is an ancient strain of wheat that is high in protein and very flavorful. The flour makes a dense and delicious pasta simply prepared with fresh seasonal vegetables. One of my favorite shapes is the twisted double strands of gemelli, or twins, produced by Rustichella d'Abruzzo.

1 eggplant, cut lengthwise into 1/4-inch-thick slices

Sea salt for dehydrating eggplant

Olive oil

1 red bell pepper, halved and seeded

1 yellow bell pepper, halved and seeded

1 red onion, quartered

2 zucchini, cut lengthwise into 1/4-inch-thick slices

8 ounces farro pasta

12 ounces ricotta cheese, lightly beaten

5 to 6 small whole leaves of fresh basil, julienned

Sea salt and freshly ground black pepper

Preheat a grill or broiler.

Sprinkle the eggplant slices with salt on both sides and let drain for 30 minutes on a wire rack. Pat dry with paper towels. Brush lightly with olive oil.

Grill or broil the vegetables on both sides until lightly browned, and transfer to a baking pan and place in the oven to keep warm.

In a large pot of salted boiling water, cook the pasta according to package directions, until al dente. Drain and toss with the ricotta cheese and basil. Season with salt and pepper. Divide the pasta among 4 serving bowls. Garnish each bowl with assorted grilled vegetables and serve at once.

Serves 4

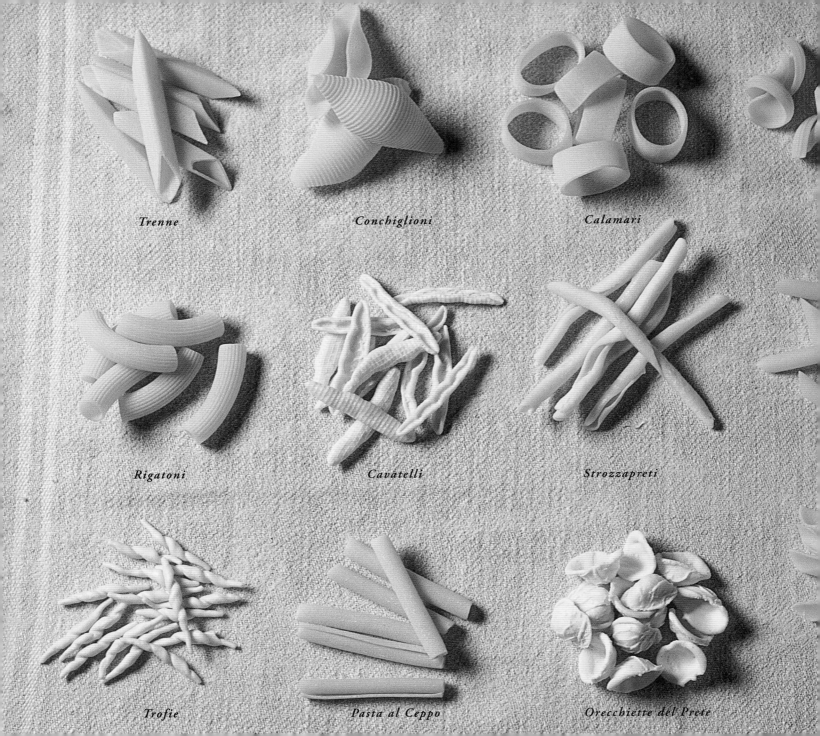

Trenne

Conchiglioni

Calamari

Rigatoni

Cavatelli

Strozzapreti

Trofie

Pasta al Ceppo

Orecchiette del Prete

Torchio

Orrechie

Penne

Cannolicchi

Garganelli

Farfalle

The South

"If flour is silver, semolina is gold."

NATIONAL MUSEUM OF PASTA, ROME

Trenne al Limone

Trenne with Lemon

This lemony pasta is ideal for seafood. Trenne is a dried, triangular tube pasta invented by Gianluigi Peduzzi of Rustichella d'Abruzzo. The name plays on the words penne and triangolo. He also makes a smaller version called trennette. You can use any tube pasta for this recipe.

1/4 cup olive oil, plus oil for grilling

1 onion, peeled and coarsely chopped

1 lemon, thinly sliced and seeded

Juice of 1 lemon

1 cup chicken stock (page 106)

1 pound trenne pasta

2 tablespoons capers, drained

1/4 cup minced fresh flat-leaf parsley

Sea salt and freshly ground black pepper

4 tuna steaks, 6 ounces each

Preheat a grill or broiler.

In a large skillet over medium heat, heat the olive oil and sauté the onion until softened, but not browned, about 3 to 4 minutes. Add the lemon slices and cook until softened, about 2 to 3 minutes. Deglaze the pan with the lemon juice. Reduce heat to a simmer and add the chicken stock. Continue to cook, uncovered, over low heat for 10 minutes, until slightly reduced.

In a large pot of salted boiling water, cook the pasta according to package directions, until al dente. Toss with the onion-lemon mixture; add the capers, parsley, and salt and pepper to taste. Keep warm.

Brush the tuna with olive oil and season with salt and pepper. Grill or broil for 4 to 5 minutes on each side, or until lightly browned on the outside, but still rare on the inside. Serve the pasta topped with a piece of grilled tuna. *Serves 4*

Maccheroni alla Chitarra Arrabiata

Pasta Made with a Chitarra in a Spicy Tomato Sauce

The chitarra is a pasta-making instrument that looks like a guitar, a rectangular wooden frame strung with wires (see page 20). If you don't have a chitarra, cut 1/4-inch strands with a sharp thin-bladed knife.

1 1/4 cup unbleached all-purpose flour

1 1/4 cup finely ground semolina

4 eggs

3 tablespoons extra-virgin olive oil

3 large cloves garlic, minced

1 peperoncino (dry red chile) or

1 teaspoon crushed red pepper flakes

1 (28-ounce) can whole tomatoes, drained and

coarsely chopped

2 tablespoons minced flat-leaf parsley

1 tablespoon minced fresh basil

Sea salt and freshly ground black pepper

On a wooden work surface, combine the flour and semolina. Make a well in the center and add the eggs. With your fingers, use a circular motion to gradually blend the eggs into the flour. Gather the dough into a ball and knead by hand for 10 to 15 minutes, or until smooth and elastic. Set aside to rest for 15 minutes.

Roll the dough into 1/4-inch-thick sheets. Place each sheet on top of the *chitarra,* and roll it with a rolling pin to press the dough through the wires, creating long noodles. Set aside on a lightly floured dish towel.

In a sauté pan over medium-high heat, heat the olive oil. Sauté the garlic and peperoncino until softened, but not brown, about 2 to 3 minutes. Add the tomatoes, parsley, and basil. Reduce to a simmer and cook for 10 to 15 minutes, until sauce is slightly thickened. Season with salt and pepper.

In a large pot of salted boiling water, cook the pasta for 4 to 5 minutes, until al dente. Drain and transfer to a warmed serving bowl. Top with the sauce and serve at once. *Serves 6*

Ziti al Forno

Oven-Baked Ziti

This is the perfect dish for a family gathering. Assemble it the day before and bake it when the guests arrive.

SAUCE

1/2 cup extra-virgin olive oil

1 clove garlic, minced

1 onion, diced

1 carrot, peeled and diced

1 stalk celery, diced

1 pound ripe tomatoes, peeled (page 107),

seeded, and coarsely chopped

2 cups veal stock (page 107)

Sea salt and freshly ground pepper to taste

MEATBALLS

3/4 pound ground veal

1 egg

3/4 cup freshly grated Parmigiano-Reggiano cheese

2 tablespoons minced fresh flat-leaf parsley

1 slice day-old country-style bread, soaked in 1/2 cup milk

Sea salt and freshly ground black pepper

Unbleached all-purpose flour for dredging

Olive oil for frying

1 pound ziti

Preheat the oven to 375°. Lightly oil a 13 by 9-inch casserole.

To make the sauce: In a large skillet over medium-high heat, warm the olive oil. Add the garlic, onion, carrot, and celery and sauté about 3 to 4 minutes. Add the tomatoes and the veal stock, stir well, reduce the heat to low, cover, and cook until slightly thickened, about 1 hour. Season with salt and pepper. Remove from the heat.

To make the meatballs: In a bowl, combine the ground meat, egg, 1/2 cup Parmigiano-Reggiano, parsley, and milk-soaked bread. Season with salt and pepper. Shape into balls 3/4 inch in diameter. Roll lightly in flour.

In a skillet over medium-high heat, warm the olive oil. Add the meatballs and cook, turning until browned, about 8 to 10 minutes. Using a slotted spoon, remove to paper towels to drain.

In a large pot of salted boiling water, cook the pasta for 8 minutes. Drain and return to the pot and toss with the sauce and the meatballs. Transfer to the prepared casserole dish. Sprinkle with the remaining 1/2 cup Parmigiano-Reggiano and bake for 30 minutes, or until the cheese has lightly browned. Serve at once. *Serves 8*

Fusilli Lunghi con Salsicce e Olive

Curly Pasta with Sausage and Olives

This is my daughter's favorite pasta shape. She loves the long curly noodles, that look like ringlets of hair.

1/4 cup extra-virgin olive oil, plus 3 tablespoons

1/4 cup lightly packed basil leaves

2 red bell peppers, roasted, peeled, and julienned

2 yellow bell peppers, roasted, peeled, and julienned

1 pound Italian sausage, cut into 1-inch lengths

1 cup pitted, oil-cured black Italian olives

1 pound fusilli or the pasta of your choice

In a blender, combine 1/4 cup olive oil and the basil. Process until the basil is completely blended. Transfer to a mixing bowl. Add the julienned peppers and set aside.

In a sauté pan over medium-high heat, heat the remaining olive oil and brown the sausages 2 minutes on each side. Add the pepper mixture and olives and heat through. Keep warm over a low heat.

In a large pot of salted boiling water, cook the pasta according to package directions, until al dente. Drain and toss with the sauce. Serve at once. *Serves 6*

Conchiglione Ripiena

Pasta Shells Stuffed with Ricotta with Sweet Peppers and Anchovy Sauce

This dish is found all across the south, with varying sizes of shells. In Italian, when you see the suffix "-one", it refers to a large size.

18 large pasta shells, cooked and drained well

FILLING

1 pound spinach, cooked, squeezed dry, and chopped

1 pound ricotta

2 egg yolks

1/4 cup freshly grated Parmigiano-Reggiano cheese

Nutmeg to taste

Sea salt and freshly ground black pepper

SAUCE

3 tablespoons extra-virgin olive oil

2 cloves garlic, minced

1 onion, finely chopped

2 cups chicken stock (page 106)

6 ripe plum tomatoes, peeled (page 107) and coarsely chopped

3 red bell peppers, roasted, peeled, and coarsely chopped

3 anchovy fillets

1/4 cup minced flat-leaf parsley

Sea salt and freshly ground black pepper

To make the filling: Mix the spinach and ricotta together. Add the egg yolks and Parmigiano-Reggiano. Season to taste with nutmeg, salt, and pepper.

To make the sauce: In a sauté pan over medium-high heat, heat the olive oil. Add the garlic and onion and sauté 2 to 3 minutes until soft, but not browned. Add the chicken stock, tomatoes, peppers, anchovies, and parsley and simmer until sauce has reduced and thickened, about 30 to 45 minutes. Purée the sauce in the blender and return to the pan. Season to taste with salt and pepper.

Preheat an oven to 350°. Lightly oil a 2-quart casserole dish. Spoon the filling into the cooked pasta shells and arrange the filled shells snugly in the dish. Pour the pepper sauce over the top and place casserole in the oven. Bake for 30 minutes, or until the sauce bubbles. Serve at once.

Serves 4 to 6

Spaghetti Carbonara

Spaghetti Carbonara

This is one of the dishes that came across the sea with Italian immigrants—we see it commonly in restaurants in America. The name spaghetti carbonara, "coal miner's spaghetti," originated due to the heartiness of the dish.

2 tablespoons extra-virgin olive oil

1 onion, diced

4 ounces pancetta, diced

4 egg yolks

1/2 cup heavy cream

1 cup (4 ounces) freshly grated
Parmigiano-Reggiano cheese

Sea salt and freshly ground black pepper

1 pound spaghetti

3 tablespoons minced fresh flat-leaf parsley

In a small sauté pan over medium heat, heat the olive oil and sauté the onion until softened, but not browned, about 3 minutes. Add the pancetta and cook until lightly browned. Set aside to cool slightly.

In a large bowl, beat the egg yolks, heavy cream, and the Parmigiano-Reggiano together. Add the cooled onion mixture and season with salt and pepper. Set aside.

In a large pot of salted boiling water, cook the spaghetti for 8 to 10 minutes, or until al dente. Drain the spaghetti and toss with the egg mixture until well coated. Turn into a warmed serving bowl, sprinkle with parsley, and serve immediately. *Serves 6*

Rigatoni al Sugo d'Agnello, Carciofi, e Rosmarino

Pasta with Lamb, Artichoke, and Rosemary Sauce

This dish is an excellent hearty main course or a sumptuous offering for an Easter brunch buffet.

5 baby artichokes

1 lemon, cut in half

1 pound boneless lamb sirloin

Sea salt and freshly ground black pepper

1/4 cup extra-virgin olive oil

1 small onion, sliced thin

1 cup red wine

2 cups veal stock (page 107)

1 (12-ounce) can whole tomatoes

1 tablespoon minced fresh flat-leaf parsley

3 sprigs of fresh rosemary

1/2 cup black Italian olives, pitted

1 pound rigatoni

Trim the tops of the artichokes. Remove the coarse outer leaves. Cut the artichokes in quarters lengthwise. Rub all cut surfaces with lemon. Squeeze the lemon into a bowl of water and let artichokes stand in the lemon water.

Cut the lamb into 1-inch cubes and season with salt and pepper. In a skillet, heat the olive oil over medium-high heat and cook the lamb cubes and onion for 8 to 10 minutes, or until the lamb is browned. Deglaze the pan with the wine, stirring to loosen any cooked particles from the pan. Reduce over high heat by one-half.

Add the stock and tomatoes (with their juices) and return to a boil. Reduce to a simmer; add the prepared artichokes, parsley, and rosemary. Cook, covered, until the artichokes are tender, about 45 to 50 minutes more. Stir in the olives and season with salt and pepper. Remove the lid and keep warm over a simmer as the pasta cooks.

In a large pot of salted boiling water, cook the pasta according to package directions, until al dente. Toss the pasta with the sauce and transfer to a warmed serving dish. Serve at once. *Serves 6*

Cannelloni

Cannelloni

Here is another of the classic southern Italian dishes that Americans know. I usually double this recipe and invite a group of friends to come for dinner.

FILLING

3/4 pound boneless veal

1 medium onion, diced

2 tablespoons olive oil

2 ounces pancetta, minced

12 ounces spinach, blanched (page 107),

squeezed dry, and chopped

3/4 cup freshly grated Parmigiano-Reggiano cheese

Sea salt and freshly ground black pepper

Fresh Pasta Dough (page 31)

BALSAMELLA

1/4 cup finely minced onion

2 tablespoons olive oil

3 tablespoons flour

3 cups milk

Sea salt and freshly ground white pepper

Freshly ground nutmeg to taste

To make the filling: In a food processor, finely chop the veal and onion. Set aside.

In a medium sauté pan, heat the olive oil. Add the pancetta and the processed meat mixture and cook over medium heat until browned, about 8 to 10 minutes. Stir in the spinach and 1/2 cup of the Parmigiano-Reggiano. Season with salt and pepper to taste. Set aside to cool.

Roll the pasta to the second thinnest setting. Cut the strips into eighteen 3-inch by 4-inch rectangles. Set aside on a lightly floured work surface.

To make the balsamella: Sauté onion in olive oil until softened, but not browned. Add the flour and cook over low heat for 3 minutes, stirring constantly. Add the milk and simmer, stirring until thickened, about 3 to 4 minutes longer. Season to taste with salt, pepper, and nutmeg.

Add 1 cup of the balsamella to the meat mixture.

In a large pot of salted boiling water, cook the pasta rectangles for 3 to 5 minutes, until just barely tender. Do not overcook. Remove from the boiling water into a large bowl of cold water to cool. Drain and place on a clean dish towel until ready to use.

Preheat the oven to 400°. Lightly oil a 13 by 9-inch baking dish. Spoon a thin layer of the balsamella into the bottom.

To assemble the cannelloni: On the long edge of one of the pasta rectangles place 2 or 3 heaping spoonfuls of the meat mixture . Roll up the rectangle into a cylinder and place in the prepared baking dish, seam side down. Repeat with the remaining squares and meat mixture, packing the rolls snugly into the dish. Cover the rolls with the remaining balsamella. Sprinkle with the remaining Parmigiano-Reggiano and bake for 20 to 25 minutes, until the Parmigiano-Reggiano has lightly browned. Serve at once. *Serves 6*

Pasta al Ceppo con Salsa di Porcini

Pasta with Wild Mushroom Sauce

The sides of these long tubes curl into each other, forming a pocket to grab a good sauce.
This autumn recipe is a savory main-dish pasta that will soothe the rumblings of the hungriest stomachs.

2 tablespoons olive oil

2 large shallots, minced

3 cloves garlic, minced

1/2 pound mixture of wild mushrooms (porcini, shiitake,
and/or chanterelle), stemmed, then sliced

2 ounces dried porcini, soaked 20 minutes in
1/2 cup warmed chicken stock (page 106)

1/4 cup marsala

2 cups chicken stock (page 106)

1 pound boneless and skinless chicken breast,
cut into julienne strips

1 teaspoon fresh thyme, minced

1 tablespoon minced flat-leaf parsley

Sea salt and freshly ground black pepper

1 pound pasta al ceppo or pasta of your choice

In a sauté pan over medium-high heat, heat the olive oil. Sauté the shallots and garlic until softened, but not browned, about 2 to 3 minutes. Add the sliced mushrooms. Strain the dried mushrooms and reserve the soaking liquid. Chop the strained mushrooms and add to the sauce. Cook for 10 minutes over medium-high heat, until softened and liquid has evaporated.

Deglaze the pan with marsala. Reduce until thickened. Add the chicken stock and reserved mushroom-soaking liquid and bring to a boil. Add the chicken, thyme, and parsley and simmer, covered, for 18 to 20 minutes, until chicken is cooked and sauce has thickened slightly. Season with salt and pepper and keep warm.

In a large pot of salted boiling water, cook the pasta according to package directions, until al dente. Drain and turn into a warmed serving bowl, spoon the sauce over the top, and serve at once. *Serves 6*

Timballo di Maccheroni con Melanzane

Eggplant and Pasta Timbale

A dish this elaborate is usually made for festive occasions, such as a holiday or birthday.
It is an impressive and delicious preparation.

3 eggplants, cut lengthwise into 1/4-inch-thick slices

Sea salt

3 tablespoons extra-virgin olive oil, plus oil to
brush eggplant and toss with pasta

1 onion, minced

1 pound lean ground beef

1 cup red wine

3 large tomatoes, peeled (page 107) and
coarsely chopped

1 tablespoon minced fresh flat-leaf parsley

1 teaspoon minced fresh rosemary

1 teaspoon minced fresh thyme

Freshly ground black pepper

1 pound annelini or other small pasta

1/4 cup freshly grated Parmigiano-Reggiano cheese

6 ounces smoked provolone cheese, sliced

Preheat a grill or broiler.

Sprinkle the eggplant slices with salt on both sides and let drain for 30 minutes on a wire rack. Pat dry with paper towels. Brush lightly with olive oil. Grill or broil the eggplant on both sides until lightly browned. Set aside.

In a large skillet, heat 3 tablespoons olive oil and sauté the onion 2 to 3 minutes until softened, but not browned. Add the ground beef and cook 4 to 5 minutes, until lightly browned. Deglaze the pan with the wine, stirring to loosen any cooked particles from the pan. Reduce over high heat until thickened. Add the tomatoes and herbs; lower the heat to a simmer. Cook, uncovered, for 15 to 20 minutes, until thickened. Season with salt and pepper.

In a large pot of salted boiling water, cook the pasta according to package directions. Drain, toss with olive oil, stir into the sauce, and set aside.

Preheat an oven to 350°. Lightly oil a 10 by 2 1/2-inch (6-cup) ring mold.

Line the prepared ring mold with the grilled eggplant slices by laying each piece side by side across the ring so that it covers the sides and bottom of the pan. Place half of the pasta mixture in the lined pan, pressing to lightly pack it. Sprinkle the pasta with the Parmigiano-Reggiano and cover with a layer of the sliced cheese. Top the cheese with the remaining pasta mixture, pressing lightly. Cover the top with a layer of eggplant. Cover the ring with parchment and seal with foil.

Bake for 30 minutes. Remove the foil and parchment paper. Invert the ring onto a platter and let stand for 5 minutes before removing the mold. Slice with a serrated knife to serve. *Serves 6*

Spaghetti con Bottarga
Spaghetti with Bottarga

Bottarga is a tasty condiment, made from dried mullet or tuna roe. It comes in a small hard brick that can easily be grated onto freshly cooked pasta. See Resources, page 108, for an importer.

1/4 cup olive oil

3 cloves garlic, minced

1/2 cup dry bread crumbs

2 tablespoons minced flat-leaf parsley

2 tablespoons salt-cured capers, rinsed and drained

1 pound spaghetti

Sea salt and freshly ground black pepper

1 ounce bottarga, grated

In a sauté pan over medium heat, heat the olive oil. Add the garlic and sauté 1 to 2 minutes until softened, but not browned. Add the bread crumbs and cook for 3 to 4 minutes, until the bread crumbs are golden brown. Stir in the parsley and capers. Set aside.

In a large pot of salted boiling water, cook the pasta according to package directions, until al dente. Drain and toss the pasta with the bread crumb mixture. Season with salt and pepper to taste. Transfer to a warmed serving bowl, sprinkle the bottarga on top, and serve at once. *Serves 6*

Strozzapreti ai Gamberi e Zucchine

Pasta with Shrimp and Zucchini

This recipe is adapted from pasta maker Mario Vicidomini's kitchen. The name strozzapreti shows a bit of humor. Literally it means "priest strangler," referring to its size and ability to choke someone. Even more amusing are the strozzacavalli, "horse stranglers"!

1/2 cup olive oil

2 cloves garlic, minced

1 peperoncino (dry red chile), crushed

10 ounces medium shrimp, cleaned and shells reserved

2 zucchini, sliced

2 tablespoons unsalted butter

1 small onion, chopped

1 cup white wine

1/4 cup minced flat-leaf parsley

1 pound cherry tomatoes, halved

Sea salt and freshly ground black pepper

1 pound strozzapreti or pasta of your choice

In a bowl, combine the olive oil, garlic, and peperoncino. Add the shrimp and zucchini and toss to coat well. Set aside to marinate until ready to cook.

In a skillet, melt the butter. Add the onion and shrimp shells and cook over medium-high heat until the onion is golden brown, about 3 to 5 minutes. Add the wine and reduce until thickened. Remove the shrimp shells and discard.

Add the shrimp-zucchini mixture and cook for 3 to 5 minutes, until the shrimp are pink and the zucchini has softened. Stir in the parsley and tomatoes. Season with salt and pepper to taste. Keep warm.

In a large pot of salted boiling water, cook the pasta according to package directions, until al dente. Drain and toss with the sauce. Serve at once. *Serves 6 to 8*

Cuscusu di Trapani

Couscous from Trapani

When you look at a map, it is easy to see how couscous found its way from North Africa to Sicily. Homemade couscous is prepared from ground semolina and water with a little saffron in it and is steamed in a special two-tiered pot. The steaming liquid below the couscous is the fish stew that it will be served with. Many good boxed couscous products are available in supermarkets. The pasta has already been cooked, so needs only to be rehydrated. Trapani, on the western coast of Sicily, is a port with an abundance of fresh seafood. Use firm-fleshed fish such as swordfish for this recipe. You can also add any variety of shellfish.

3 tablespoons extra-virgin olive oil

1 carrot, peeled and minced

1 stalk celery, minced

1 onion, finely chopped

2 cups dry white wine

6 cups fish stock (page 106)

1 clove garlic, minced

2 pounds boneless assorted fresh fish, cleaned and cut into 2-inch pieces

1/4 cup minced flat-leaf parsley, plus several parsley leaves for garnish

1 peperoncino (dry red chile)

Sea salt and freshly ground black pepper

12 ounces instant couscous

In a sauté pan over medium-high heat, heat the olive oil. Sauté the carrot, celery, and onion until golden brown, about 5 to 6 minutes. Deglaze the pan with the wine, stirring to loosen any cooked particles from the pan. Cook over high heat until reduced by one-half. Add the fish stock and garlic and bring to a boil. Add the fish, parsley, and peperoncino and reduce to a simmer. Cook for 8 to 10 minutes, until the fish is firm and opaque. Season to taste with salt and pepper.

Remove the fish with a slotted spoon and keep warm. Place the couscous in a large bowl and pour the fish cooking broth over it. Stir gently. Transfer to a warmed serving platter, top with the fish, and garnish with parsley leaves. Serve at once. *Serves 6*

Orecchiette con Cime di Rape

Pasta with Turnip Greens

Natalizia Rosato, the cook at the agriturismo Masseria Salamina in Puglia, makes her orecchiette with 100 percent semolina. In this version, I've substituted part of the semolina with all-purpose flour to make the dough a little easier to work with. The results are very good served with her favorite sauce, spicy turnip greens.

ORECCHIETTE

1 cup unbleached all-purpose flour

2 cups finely ground semolina

1 cup water

SAUCE

10 ounces (about 4 cups) turnip greens, julienned

3 tablespoons extra-virgin olive oil

2 cloves garlic, minced

3 anchovy fillets

2 ripe tomatoes, peeled (page 107) and coarsely chopped

1 peperoncino (dry red chile)

Sea salt and freshly ground black pepper

To make the orecchiette: Using the ingredients at left, prepare dough using the method on page 31.

Cut the dough into 4 pieces and roll each into long ropes 1/2 inch thick. With a sharp thin-bladed knife, cut each rope into small disks 1/4 inch thick. Press each disk firmly with a palette knife, smearing it flat. Turn the flattened disk over your thumb to give it a little bulge. Leave to dry on a lightly floured dish towel until ready to cook.

To make the sauce: In a large pot of boiling salted water, blanch the turnip greens (page 107). Drain and reserve the cooking water to cook the orecchiette.

In a sauté pan over medium-high heat, heat the olive oil. Add the garlic, anchovies, tomato, and peperoncino. Cook 10 minutes, then add the turnip greens and cook for 5 minutes longer, until very soft. Remove the peperoncino and season the sauce with salt and pepper. Keep warm.

Bring the cooking water back to a boil and add the oriecchiette. Cook for 3 to 4 minutes, until al dente. Drain and add to the sauce. Transfer to a warmed serving bowl and serve at once. *Serves 6*

Malloreddus

Sardinian Gnocchi with Tomato Sauce

*Malloreddus, also called gnocchetti sardi, is the name of the small gnocchi
from Sardinia. They are dense because they are made from semolina. They have a pleasant yellow color
and saffron flavor and look like an empty shell.*

MALLOREDDUS

1 1/2 cups semolina flour

Pinch of salt

Pinch of saffron, soaked in 1/2 cup warm water

Unbleached all-purpose flour

SAUCE

2 tablespoons extra-virgin olive oil

1 clove garlic, minced

1/2 cup finely chopped onion

*6 ripe plum tomatoes, peeled (page 107),
seeded, and coarsely chopped*

2 tablespoons minced fresh basil

2 tablespoons minced fresh flat-leaf parsley

2 cups chicken stock (page 106)

Sea salt and freshly ground black pepper

On a work surface, mix together the semolina and salt. Make a well and add the saffron-water. Work the water into the dough until it comes together. Knead for 10 minutes, or until smooth and firm. Roll the dough into 1/2-inch-thick ropes and cut the ropes into 1/2-inch-long pieces. Dust the pieces with the all-purpose flour and make indentations with the tines of a fork, pressing a concave impression in the opposite side with your thumb. Set aside on a lightly floured work surface.

To make the sauce: In a large, heavy saucepan over medium heat, heat the oil and sauté the garlic and onion until soft, but not brown, about 3 minutes.

Add the tomatoes, basil, parsley, and chicken stock. Simmer until the sauce has thickened, about 30 to 45 minutes. Purée the sauce in a blender and return to the pan. Season to taste with salt and pepper. Keep warm.

In a large pot of salted boiling water, cook the malloreddus until they rise to the surface, about 3 to 4 minutes. Drain and top with the sauce. *Serves 4*

Basic Recipes

CHICKEN STOCK

1 (3-pound) chicken or chicken parts, cut up

1 carrot, peeled and cut into 1/2-inch pieces

1 stalk celery, cut into 1/2-inch pieces

1 onion, cut into 1/2-inch pieces

Bouquet garni: 1 sprig of parsley, 1 bay leaf,

1 sprig of thyme, 4 to 5 black peppercorns

1 gallon (16 cups) spring water

Place all the ingredients in a large stockpot and bring to a boil. Reduce heat to a simmer and cook, uncovered, for 2 hours, periodically skimming off the foam. Strain, discarding the chicken and vegetables. Refrigerate the stock until the fat solidifies and can be removed. *Makes 5 quarts*

FISH STOCK

1/4 cup extra-virgin olive oil

2 onions, coarsely chopped

2 carrots, peeled and coarsely chopped

3 stalks celery, coarsely chopped

1/2 cup dry white wine

1 gallon (16 cups) spring water

1 pound fish bones

Bouquet garni: 1 sprig of parsley, 1 bay leaf,

1 sprig of thyme, 4 to 5 black peppercorns

In a large stockpot, heat the olive oil over medium heat and sauté the onion, carrots, and celery for 5 to 8 minutes, or until browned. Add the wine, increase the heat to high, and stir to loosen cooked particles from the bottom of the pan.

Continue cooking until the wine is almost completely evaporated. Add the water, fish bones, and bouquet garni. Bring to a boil, decrease heat to a simmer, and cook for at least 45 minutes. Strain the stock and discard the bones and vegetables. *Makes 3 quarts*

Basic Recipes

VEAL STOCK

10 pounds veal shank bones, cut into 3-inch lengths

2 onions, cut into 1-inch pieces

2 carrots, peeled and cut into 1-inch pieces

1 stalk celery, cut into 1-inch pieces

Bouquet garni: 1 sprig of parsley, 1 bay leaf,

1 sprig of thyme, 4 to 5 black peppercorns

3 gallons spring water

Preheat the oven to 425°. Put the veal bones and onions in a lightly oiled baking pan and roast for 35 to 40 minutes, or until very brown. Put the bones, onions, and all the remaining ingredients in a large stockpot and bring to a boil. Reduce heat to a simmer and cook, uncovered, for 8 hours, periodically skimming the foam from the top. Strain, discarding the solids. Refrigerate the stock until the fat solidifies and can be removed. *Makes 5 quarts*

TO TOAST NUTS

Preheat the oven to 350°. Put the nuts on a baking sheet and toast in oven for 8 to 10 minutes, or until golden brown and aromatic. Pine nuts take less time, about 5 to 7 minutes.

TO BLANCH VEGETABLES

Drop the vegetables in boiling salted water for 30 seconds; transfer immediately to ice water to stop the cooking.

TO PEEL AND SEED TOMATOES

Drop the tomatoes in boiling salted water for 30 seconds; drain in a colander until cool enough to handle. Make a small slit in the skin of each tomato and easily peel away the skins. Cut the tomatoes in half crosswise and scoop out the seeds in each section cavity with your index finger.

Resources

INGREDIENT RESOURCES BY MAIL

Balducci's
424 Avenue of the Americas
New York, NY 10011
(212) 673-2600, Catalog (800) 225-3822
Anchovies in salt or oil, artisanal pastas

Corti Brothers
PO Box 191359
Sacramento, CA 95819
(800) 509-3663
Spinosi pasta, Latini pasta

Dean & Deluca Mail Order
(800) 221-7714, Fax (800) 781-4050
www.dean-deluca-catalog.com
*Canned San Marzano tomatoes, artisanal
pastas*

Esperya USA
3 Westchester Plaza
Elmsford, NY 10523
www.esperya.com/usa
*Selectors of fine Italian products feature only
two pasta producers: Latini and Rustichella
d'Abruzzo*

Manicaretti
5332 College Avenue, No. 200
Oakland, CA 94618
(800) 799-9830
Rustichella d'Abruzzo pasta, salt-cured capers

Pasta Shop
5665 College Avenue
Oakland, CA 94618
(510) 547-4005 or 652-0462
Fax (510) 652-4669
*Fresh pasta; many artisanal dry pastas including
Rustichella d'Abruzzo and Latini*

Todaro Brothers
555 Second Avenue
New York, NY 10016
(212) 679-7766, Fax (212) 689-1679
*Canned San Marzano tomatoes, imported
mozzarella di bufala, Italian Tipo 00 flour*

Williams-Sonoma (stores nationwide)
Catalog (800) 541-2233
*Canned San Marzano tomatoes, artisanal
pastas, pasta makers*

IN ITALY

**Italian Food Artisans Wine and
Food Workshops**
1324 State Street, J-157
Santa Barbara, CA 93101
(805) 963-7289; Fax (805) 963-0230
www.FoodArtisans.com
E-mail: Pamela@FoodArtisans.com
Week-long wine and food workshops in Italy

Historical Museum of Spaghetti
Via Garibaldi, 96
10827 Pontedassio (IM)

Masseria Salamina
72010 Pezze di Greco
Fasano (BR) Puglia
Tel./Fax (011.39) 080.489.7307
E-mail: salamina@mailbox.media.it
Agriturismo, cooking classes

National Museum of Pasta
Piazza Scanderbeg, 117
00187 Rome
(011.39) 06.699.1119
Fax (011.39) 06.699.1109

Tenuta di Seliano
Cecilia Baratta Bellelli
(011.39) 0828.72.36.34
Fax (011.39) 0828.72.45.41
E-mail: seliano@amalfinet.it
Agriturismo, cooking classes

FOR FURTHER REFERENCE

Anderson, Burton. *Treasures of the Italian Table*.
New York: William Morrow, 1994.

Ballerini, Luigi, "The Origins of Pasta," *La
Cucina Italiana,* May–June 2000.

Il Buon Paese. Bra, Italy: Slow Food, 1994.

Field, Carol. *The Italian Baker*. New York:
HarperCollins, 1985.

Jenkins, Nancy Harmon. *Flavors of Puglia*.
New York: Broadway Books, 1997.

——. *Flavors of Tuscany*. New York: Broadway
Books, 1998.

Johns, Pamela Sheldon. *Italian Food Artisans*.
San Francisco: Chronicle Books, 1999.

The National Museum of Pasta. *Pasta in
Museum*. Rome: Istituto Poligrafico e Zecca
dello Stato, 1999.

——. *Time for Pasta*. Rome: Istituto Poligrafico
e Zecca dello Stato, 1999.

Acknowledgments

Pamela Sheldon Johns would like to thank my dear friends in Italy, Lucy De Fazio, Cecilia Baratta Bellelli, and Kimberly Wicks Bartolozzi, for their invaluable help with research and logistics in Italy. Thanks to each of the artisans: Giuseppina Maffia, Natalizia Rosato, Anna Luigia Leone, Luciana di Giandomenico, the Martelli family, and especially Gianluigi Peduzzi and his family. Grazie mille to Ed Valenzuela and Manicaretti Imports for providing us with excellent dried pasta for testing and photos. Much appreciation back at home to my friends who helped with recipe testing and other details: Judy Dawson, Philippa Farrar, Michelle Holmes, Brynn Stotko, Stacey Tillotson, Julie Boyer, Jaana Vaatainen, Tom Beidler. Alaia and I wish to express our appreciation to our traveling companion and photographer Joyce Oudkerk-Pool. Kisses to Courtney, the ultimate pasta recipe taster.

Tremendous thanks and appreciation to the generous collaboration of Jennifer Barry, a great partner and friend.

Jennifer Barry Design would like to thank the following individuals and establishments for their support of this book project: Ten Speed publisher Kirsty Melville and editorial director Lorena Jones for giving us the opportunity to publish another cookbook in our Italian series so that we can continue to share our love of Italian food with cooks around the world; Joyce Oudkerk-Pool for traveling to Italy again to photograph the wonderful artisanal pasta producers featured in the book, and for her stunning recipe photography produced with the help of our favorite food stylist Pouké Halpern, we are most appreciative; Carol Hacker for providing us with beautiful, authentic Italian props; Barbara King for her editing skill; and Kristen Wurz for her tranquil presence and unerring production expertise.

To my collaborator Pamela Sheldon Johns, thank you for sharing your love and knowledge of all things Italian. Your spirit, generosity, and culinary skill are a constant source of inspiration!

Index

ALSO BY THE AUTHORS IN THIS SERIES

Balsamico!
A Balsamic Vinegar Cookbook

Gelato!
Italian Ice Creams, Sorbetti & Granite

Parmigiano!
50 New & Classic Recipes with Parmigiano-Reggiano Cheese

Pizza Napoletana!